OPPORTUNITIES

in

P9-DFB-684

Holistic Health Care Careers

REVISED EDITION

GILLIAN TIERNEY

McGraw Hill

New York   Chicago   San Francisco   Lisbon   London   Madrid   Mexico City
Milan   New Delhi   San Juan   Seoul   Singapore   Sydney   Toronto

The McGraw·Hill Companies

Library of Congress Cataloging-in-Publication Data

Tierney, Gillian.
   Opportunities in holistic health care careers / by Gillian Tierney. — Rev. ed.
      p.   cm.
   ISBN 0-07-146767-X (alk. paper)
   1. Holistic medicine—Vocational guidance.   I. Title.

   R733.T54   2007
   615.5071—dc22   2006014339

1 2 3 4 5 6 7 8 9 10 11 12 13 14 15 16 17 18 19   DOC/DOC   0 9 8 7 6

ISBN-13: 978-0-07-146767-4
ISBN-10:   0-07-146767-X

Interior design by Rattray Design

McGraw-Hill books are available at special quantity discounts to use as premiums and sales promotions, or for use in corporate training programs. For more information, please write to the Director of Special Sales, Professional Publishing, McGraw-Hill, Two Penn Plaza, New York, NY 10121-2298. Or contact your local bookstore.

This book is printed on acid-free paper.

For Bettina

CONTENTS

qualifications. Salary and job outlook. Professional
organizations. Schools.

conditions. The profession. Training and
qualifications. Salary and job outlook. Professional
organizations. Schools.

Foreword

Opportunities for rewarding careers in holistic health care have never been greater and will only continue to expand. One important reason is the growing appreciation and acceptance by the general public of the value of holistic approaches to both health and well-being. Approximately 40 percent of Americans now use some form of alternative or complementary medicine in place of or to supplement the care they receive from mainstream health care providers, such as their physicians.

Conventional medicine excels in emergency medicine and in heroic measures such as surgery, but it is ill-equipped to understand and effectively work with today's chronic and degenerative diseases. Holistic approaches, on the other hand, have a great deal to offer for these conditions and will be increasingly in demand as our population lives longer and confronts the challenges of aging.

Another reason for the popularity of holistic and alternative health care is that people are becoming increasingly wary of the dangers of conventional medicine, and rightfully so. Recent findings reported in the *Journal of the American Medical Association* raised eyebrows when they revealed that adverse effects from conventional treatments (unnecessary surgeries, medication, and other errors in hospitals; hospital-acquired infections; and the adverse effects of medications) may be the third-leading cause of death in America, following heart disease and cancer.

Today's health care consumer wants alternatives and wants to be treated as a whole person, not merely a person with a disease. We are much more than blood chemistry, bones, and cellular tissue. We are beings of energy and spirit as well. We are complex, multisystemic beings, and the symptoms of illness have meaning only within this larger context, not in isolation.

I have been practicing and teaching in this field for many years, and I can tell you from direct experience that patients genuinely appreciate being treated by a practitioner who has a holistic perspective. It is extremely gratifying to witness a patient with cancer turn his or her illness around and defeat the odds by taking a holistic approach. It is no less exciting to hear the news that a heart patient has saved himself or herself from bypass surgery by successfully following a holistic approach to heart health. Such stories are becoming more and more commonplace. I invite you to explore this exciting field and find your place within it, so that you, too, can enjoy the rich personal rewards of this service.

William Collinge, Ph.D., M.P.H.
Author of *The American Holistic Health Association Complete Guide to Alternative Medicine* and *Subtle Energy*

Preface

ACCORDING TO RECENT government statistics, health care, which is the largest industry in the United States, provides approximately 13.5 million jobs. These include the following professionals:

Chiropractors
Clinical laboratory technologists and technicians
Dentists and dental hygienists
Dietitians and nutritionists
Emergency medical technicians and paramedics
Optometrists
Pharmacists
Physician assistants
Physicians and surgeons
Podiatrists
Psychologists and psychiatrists
Registered nurses
Social workers

These are all health care providers working in some facet of mainstream health care. The settings in which these professionals work include hospitals; nursing and residential care facilities; offices of physicians, dentists, and other health practitioners; outpatient care centers; and medical and diagnostic laboratories.

These impressive statistics are misleading, however, because they fail to consider the millions of additional health care providers working in the fields of holistic health care and complementary and alternative medicine (CAM). Holistic health care professionals practice in equally wide-ranging fields, including the following:

Acupuncture
Ayurveda
Biofeedback
Chelation therapy
Chiropractic care
Energy healing therapy
Folk medicine
Guided imagery
Homeopathic treatment
Hypnosis
Massage therapy
Meditation
Naturopathy
Qigong
Reiki
Tai chi
Yoga

These health care providers work in hospitals, offices, gyms, spas, retreats, and group practices. Typically, the settings in which they work are more varied and less clinical than those of mainstream health care providers, although the two areas of health care are increasingly combining strengths and working together to improve people's health and wellness.

How do you find out information about specific health care jobs, both mainstream and holistic? If you want to become a doctor, nurse, physical therapist, or pharmacist, the resources are endless. There is no shortage of career manuals, websites, articles, and advisers full of advice for these well-known careers. What about the aspiring acupuncturist? Where is the budding herbalist or massage therapist to turn? Although increasing in numbers over the past ten years, there are not a lot of resources for these potential future holistic health care providers. The dearth of information available for these people is what motivated me to write the first edition of this book. While information about and appreciation for these career paths have grown in recent years, alternative health care careers remain overlooked. This book is my attempt to bring these rewarding careers into consideration for those searching for a health care career. I hope you find this a refreshing addition to your career planning!

Acknowledgments

I would like to thank the following health care practitioners who were kind enough to share information and personal insights about their professions: Jennifer Jennings, Marj MacLaughlin, Leslie Newman, Lisa Rothermich, Ranan Cohen, Dayton Haigney, Leon Hecht III, Kristy Fassler, Bernard Schechter, Ann Ernish, Rebecca Petee, Cilia Bannenberg, Tim Kingsbury, and Katherine Evans. I also thank William Collinge for the wonderful foreword and Suzan Walter, Barry Delin, and Dave Molony for sharing their resources. Thanks to Susan Holden and Sam Allen from St. Anselm College for all their encouragement and support. A special thank you to my husband, George Shea, for increasing my interest in writing and for his never-ending support of all my endeavors.

1

WHAT IS HOLISTIC
HEALTH CARE?

HOLISTIC HEALTH, HOLISTIC medicine, alternative medicine, complementary medicine . . . what do they all mean? There is confusion over the meaning of the word *holistic* because there is no standard definition, and many of these terms get used interchangeably. Here we will attempt to clarify the meaning of holistic health and lay the foundation for the career areas that follow. Holistic health is not one specific career but a unique way of viewing health and illness.

Holistic health is a philosophy concerned with the well-being of the whole person—body, mind, and spirit. The word *holistic* is derived from the word *holism*. The concept of holism states that living organisms are made up of constantly interacting independent elements, in which the whole is greater than the sum of its parts. Holistic health care looks at the whole person and recognizes that health is influenced by many interacting elements: body, mind, spirit, family, diet, genetics, emotions, lifestyle, and environment.

1

The entire human experience is appreciated. Holistic health is not a specific method of treatment, but an overall view of treatment and health. When holistic philosophies are applied to health problems, the process is often termed *holistic medicine*. The American Holistic Medical Association defines holistic medicine this way:

> Holistic medicine is the art and science of healing that addresses the whole person—body, mind, and spirit. The practice of holistic medicine integrates conventional and alternative therapies to prevent and treat disease, and most importantly, to promote optimal health. This condition of holistic health is defined as the unlimited and unimpeded free flow of life force energy through body, mind, and spirit. Holistic medicine encompasses all safe and appropriate modalities of diagnosis and treatment. It includes analysis of physical, nutritional, environmental, emotional, spiritual and lifestyle elements. Holistic medicine focuses upon patient education and participation in the healing process.

The holistic view of health and wellness is quite different from conventional, traditional, mainstream, or allopathic medicine. For the purpose of this book, these words are used interchangeably and refer to the more popular mainstream medicine practiced by most M.D.s. The conventional medical model emphasizes the study, diagnosis, and treatment of a disease. As a group, traditional medicine focuses on the specific diseased part of the body. Its strength is in acute trauma care, such as emergency medicine and necessary surgery.

Holistic practitioners focus on health; practitioners of conventional medicine typically focus on disease. Holistic health care providers believe in the body's own natural healing abilities and focus on supporting the body in its healing process. Holistic medicine's greatest strengths are maintaining health and wellness, disease prevention, and treatment of chronic, degenerative conditions, many of which are not addressed by mainstream medicine. Its practitioners prefer to use less-invasive methods of care primarily by using natural, nontoxic remedies as opposed to pharmaceutical treatments. Holistic care includes not only working with the physical body, but also with mental, emotional, and spiritual factors to provide comprehensive care to the whole person. The holistic model believes health is not reached by the elimination of disease but is a constantly changing state that must be actively maintained. Holistic practitioners emphasize preventive care to reduce risk of illness and to maximize health potential. Their goal is to achieve optimum health and vitality—to help patients feel healthy, energetic, and clear minded and have an overall sense of wellness.

Symptoms of illness are viewed differently in the holistic philosophy. They are seen as the body's way to communicate problems; useful signals that something is wrong. Holistic health practitioners use symptoms to find the underlying causes of health problems. They attempt to treat the source of symptoms rather than focus on eliminating particular symptoms. For example, if a patient has a headache, the holistic practitioner will search to find the underlying cause of this symptom, such as identifying stressors and recommending exercises or meditation to prevent future headaches; they will not simply prescribe a pill to treat the current headache.

Central to the concept of holistic health is empowerment. The patient or client is viewed as the one responsible for his or her health. Holistic health practitioners see their role as teachers, working to educate patients on how they can improve and take control of their health. The practitioner and client work together to solve health problems, and patients are trusted and encouraged to make health decisions. The practitioner is a cofacilitator of health rather than an authority figure. This model increases patients' investment, control, and ownership of health and can increase their natural healing powers by reducing feelings of helplessness. It can be motivating for patients to realize they can do something to improve their health and don't have to wholly rely on others.

Who Practices Holistic Health Care?

Any health care practitioner, including mainstream medical practitioners, can have a holistic philosophy. For example, increasingly, doctors and dentists are applying holistic tenets to their practice, and nursing—an area that has embraced holism to varying degrees throughout its history—is moving toward embracing its roots in holism. This book, however, specifically examines health care careers that always practice using a holistic philosophy. Health care practitioners who believe in a holistic philosophy often offer alternative forms of health care, thus the term *alternative medicine*. This book could have been titled *Opportunities in Alternative Medicine*. Alternative medicine is frequently holistic but describes all forms of health care outside of mainstream medicine. For the purpose of this book, we assume the alternative methods of care follow a holistic philosophy. It is important to remember that not all alternative health care practitioners are holistic, and not all holistic practitioners are alternative—it is a question of the health care provider's philosophy toward health.

Differences Between Holistic Health Care and Traditional Medicine

Are the areas of focus between holistic and mainstream health care providers really so different? And what are these differences anyway? At this point, you're probably asking yourself these questions. The differences between these two types of practitioners lie in their

Table 1.1 Comparison of the Practice of Holistic Health Care and Traditional Medicine

Holistic Health Care	*Traditional Medicine*
Focuses on the whole person (mind, body, spirit)	Focuses on diseased body part
Focuses on health	Focuses on disease
Is preventive	Treats problems, symptoms, diseases
Believes in the body's own healing abilities	Believes healing comes from external sources
Uses nontoxic, natural remedies	Uses drugs and surgical procedures
Believes patient is responsible for health	Believes care provider is responsible for health
Considers care provider a cofacilitator and teacher	Considers care provider an authority figure
Treats underlying causes	Treats symptoms
Interprets symptoms as signals that something is wrong	Considers symptoms something to stop
Goal: to achieve optimum level of wellness	Goal: to achieve absence of disease

philosophy and the focus of their practice. Their philosophy guides their work on a daily basis. Table 1.1 illustrates these differences. As you will see, they are quite substantial.

Words of Advice

The information provided in this book comes from careful research and study, yet, because the field is rapidly growing and changing, some newer career paths may not be discussed. Conduct extensive research on your own, both online and in a library, to ensure you're making the best holistic health care career choice. Librarians are a particularly good source of information, and they can lead you to other books or magazines on the topic.

In addition to reading about your career options, spend time with practitioners who have careers that interest you. Ask a practitioner if you can shadow or observe him or her during a typical day. Or, ask if you can have an informational interview that lasts no more than one hour. Come prepared with a list of questions, and bring a notepad to write down information. Most people will be flattered that you're taking an interest in their work, and they'll be happy to encourage a future holistic health care provider to enter the field.

Before you commit to an area of study or school, carefully research training programs and consider your options thoroughly. The schools listed in this book are schools that were accessible due to their marketing, advertising, and reputation, which means that these are not complete lists, and there are many schools omitted. The inclusion of a school does not indicate my endorsement or support but is meant to give you a start in locating training programs. Every program is different and must be evaluated on its own merits. Visit the campus and talk to professors or guidance counselors before committing to a program.

About This Book

Each of the chapters in the book will discuss the philosophy, types of problems/patients, methods of care, working conditions, training requirements, salary, and employment outlook for each occupation. For some career areas the holistic philosophy is embedded in the care. For others it is more loosely applied. All forms of holistic care share in the effort to help people find new, less-toxic, natural approaches to healing.

Although this book demonstrates the value and need for holistic health care practitioners, it isn't intended to imply that conventional medicine is unethical, ineffective, or unnecessary. Both conventional and holistic health care have their strengths and weaknesses and are necessary parts of the health care system in this country. The career areas included here provide an alternative health career option. Medicine is a science and an art, with many different paths to healing. The holistic health care careers add breadth to the field of health care by providing new and different approaches to health. It is an exciting time to join this dynamic and growing field. Best of luck in finding the health care career that works for you!

Sources of Additional Information

American Holistic Health Association
www.ahha.org

American Holistic Medical Association
www.ahma.org

American Holistic Nurses Association
www.ahna.org

American Integrative Medical Association
http://aihcp-norfolkva.org/AIMA

Association for Integrative Health Care Practitioners
http://aihcp-norfolkva.org/AIHCP

Global Institute for Alternative Medicine
www.gifam.org

Holistic Pediatric Association
www.hpakids.org

National Center for Complementary and Alternative Medicine
http://nccam.nih.gov

2

ACUPUNCTURE AND TRADITIONAL CHINESE MEDICINE

TRADITIONAL CHINESE MEDICINE is the common name for a group of healing practices used for over three thousand years to prevent and treat disease by restoring balance and harmony to the total person: body, mind, and spirit. Chinese medicine views health as part of the natural world. Health depends on mental and physical harmony as well as harmony with nature. Acupuncture, often considered synonymous with Chinese medicine, has been practiced in the United States for more than 150 years. It is the gentle and virtually painless insertion of hair-fine needles into specific points on the body to stimulate the body's natural healing abilities. Most of this chapter will focus on acupuncture because that is the aspect of Chinese medicine most people in the United States pursue.

While traditional Chinese medicine is considered part of alternative health care in the West, it is still widely practiced, alongside more familiar modern treatments, in China and other parts of the East. Indeed, the modern practice of traditional Chinese medicine is increasingly incorporating techniques and theories of Western medicine. In recent decades, there has also been an effort to integrate the discoveries made by traditional Chinese medicine with those of mainstream Western medical traditions. One important component of this work is to use the instrumentation and the methodological tools to research and investigate observations made and hypotheses raised by the Chinese tradition. Western studies have shown Chinese medicine to be effective in treating a variety of health problems, including migraines, nausea and vomiting associated with chemotherapy and pregnancy, and other forms of pain.

Philosophy

Traditional Chinese medicine is based on the idea that the human body is a small universe with a set of complete and sophisticated interconnected systems. These systems usually work in balance to maintain the healthy function of the human body, and they include qi, blood, jing, bodily fluids, the wu xing, emotions, and spirit (shen). *Qi* or *chi* (pronounced "chee") is the life energy that flows throughout the body. Illness is defined as a disharmony, blockage, deficiency, or imbalance of qi. The qi flows through the body along fourteen main pathways called meridians. Certain key points (acupuncture points) on the body correspond to organ systems. By stimulating these points, an acupuncturist seeks to increase the flow of qi to relieve pain, treat disease, and resolve problems on the most fundamental, energetic level.

When acupuncturists work with clients, they view the body in an entirely different way from practitioners of Western medicine. First, they view symptoms as signs of a deeper problem or a lack of balance in the body. Rather than merely treating the symptom, acupuncturists work to treat the underlying causes of a symptom.

Second, they view health problems in terms of yin and yang theory and a person's qi or life energy. They ask, is a person's qi blocked? weak? excessive? Is there too much yin? Too little yang? The concepts of yin and yang and qi are the philosophical underpinnings of acupuncture and Chinese medicine.

Yin and *yang* are words used to describe the cycle of energy, harmony, and balance in all living things and events. Just as the seasons change, the body is a changing energy pattern that needs a balance of yin and yang for harmony. The concept of yin is considered the feminine principle and refers to complete, solid, and permanent states. Yang is the masculine principle referring to moving, changing, dynamic states. In the body, yin refers to tissues and organs and yang to the body's activities and functions. Even specific organs are divided into yin and yang groups. Yin organs are the more solid organs such as the heart, kidney, liver, and lungs. Yang organs are the more fluid and changing organs through which materials pass such as the stomach, bladder, and intestines. The philosophy holds that when yin and yang are out of balance, health problems occur.

Types of Clients and Problems

Acupuncture is great for treating a broad range of problems. I like being able to affect a person's health and well-being in a way that doesn't have adverse side effects. It's more than the specific thing I am working on—acupuncture treats their sore back, but in addition people feel good and often their energy will improve. It gives people a sense of well-being.

—Lisa Rothermich, Licensed Acupuncturist

Acupuncture can be effective in areas where traditional medicine is limited. Acupuncturists specialize in the treatment of clients with chronic diseases, stress-related disorders, and pain. Acupuncturists treat patients with health problems such as:

Headaches	Migraines
Muscle pain	Allergies
Tendinitis	Diabetes
Sciatica	Stroke
Skin rashes	Bladder dysfunction
Back pain	Arthritis
Asthma	Nausea
Toothaches	Digestive problems
Colitis	Poor vision
Gum problems	Sinusitis
Colds	Premenstrual syndrome
Bronchitis	Addictions
Infertility	Menopausal symptoms
Tonsillitis	

Acupuncturists also treat various psychological problems, including depression and anxiety. People seeking help with weight control, smoking addiction, alcohol and drug addictions, and stress reduction, and other such conditions often see acupuncturists. Relaxation, increased energy, and improved immune system are inherent benefits of acupuncture.

People of all ages, from newborns to the elderly, go to acupuncturists, although more women than men seek acupuncture as a treatment method for health problems. Some people choose acupuncture as a first step toward solving health problems. Others approach acupuncture as a last resort when traditional medicine has failed or as an attempt to avoid surgery or other invasive procedures.

Types of Treatment

Those who practice Chinese medicine believe that the human body possesses the inherent potential to locate the source of illness and distribute the resources and energy necessary to heal the problems on its own, without any unnecessary interventions. To maintain a body that's healthy enough to do this, one must practice daily breathing and circulation exercises, such as qigong, tai chi, or other Chinese martial arts. If outside interventions are necessary, the goal of these efforts is to assist the normal self-healing function of the human body, not interfere with it; this usually is in the form of acupuncture. Traditional Chinese medicine uses herbs and other drugs as the last resort to combat health problems. Other specialties include nutrition or food therapy and herbal medicines, in addition to acupuncture.

There is much more to acupuncture than needles. Acupuncturists use a complex system of techniques to diagnose and treat problems. The first appointment with a patient, lasting between one and a half to three hours, consists of a detailed individual and family health history in addition to some treatment. Acupuncturists ask questions about digestive problems, urine color, menstrual cycle, eating habits, allergies, sleeping patterns, past attempted treatments, work and family life, stress level, and sensitivities to temperature. They understand that a patient's anxiety, anger, fear, and emotional/psychological stressors can influence health. During the interview, the acupuncturist will carefully observe a patient's complexion, face, tongue, body language, and tone of voice. Finally a pulse diagnosis is used to determine treatment.

In Chinese medicine there are twelve different pulses, each associated with a vital organ. The acupuncturist feels three pulses by lightly placing three fingers at each wrist. By pressing more firmly and deeply at the same three places on each wrist, three additional pulses are felt. The quality and sensations of the pulses are used to discover any problems in the flow of qi and diagnose the nature of illness.

Once a diagnosis is made, acupuncturists treat patients by inserting small, hair-fine needles into the skin at certain points in the body. The needles are carefully placed along the energy meridians to improve the flow of qi to specific organs and body parts. Typically ten to fifteen sterile surgical steel needles are left in for fifteen to forty-five minutes. Acupuncturists may slightly turn the needles once inserted to enhance their effect. In some instances, acupuncturists may connect the needles to a low-voltage electrical source to increase stimulation. Acupuncture does not hurt and has been described as a tingling sensation or a mild buzz.

Beyond needles, there are several additional techniques used in acupuncture and Chinese medicine. Although the methods vary, all share the goal of improving the flow of qi and creating balance in the body. With moxibustion, a small cone made from herbs is placed on the skin at acupuncture points and is ignited so that heat and herbs penetrate the skin without burning. Acupressure and shiatsu are methods that use massage and applying pressure to acupuncture points. Traditional Chinese medicine uses herbs in conjunction with acupuncture to treat illness. Acupuncturists may also recommend dietary modifications, herbal and vitamin supplements, specific therapeutic exercises, and lifestyle management strategies.

There are a couple of different aspects of acupuncture in practice today. *Auriculotherapy* is acupuncture of the ear relying on more than the four traditional ear acupoints. Laser acupuncture is the use of laser beams to stimulate the acupoints. Japanese acupuncture is unique in its use of even thinner needles.

Follow-up acupuncture sessions usually last one hour. The length of treatment varies, but generally a course of treatment consists of ten treatments performed over several weeks. The length depends on the overall health of a person and the presenting problem. For most problems, acupuncturists see patients once a week. Patients with severe pain may require sessions a few times a week. Treatments may take longer for patients who have a poor diet or high stress and don't get enough exercise. Acute problems such as a sprained ankle in an otherwise healthy person may need only one or two acupuncture sessions. Chronic conditions such as long-term back pain may require a series of treatments. Treatment is individualized to the patient's needs and varies from person to person.

Employment Settings and Working Conditions

I'm not interested in working five or six days a week at acupuncture. I have a small business out of my home, so my acupuncture practice is three days per week. What's nice about being self-employed is the flexibility!

—Lisa Rothermich

Almost all acupuncturists are in private practice, either individually or in a group practice. Some teach and conduct research at schools of acupuncture. Acupuncturists are increasingly finding employment in hospital settings or are working in wellness centers. Some hospitals incorporate acupuncture into substance abuse programs, while others have holistic health or integrative medical departments.

Acupuncturists may also work in group practices with other holistic health care practitioners. It is not unusual for an acupuncturist, massage therapist, nutritionist, and naturopathic physician to work together in one practice. Acupuncturists are also responsible for advertising and marketing their service to develop a clientele, and like any new business, it can take time to build up a practice.

This profession provides a good deal of flexibility and control. Acupuncturists work out of their homes or out of clean and comfortable offices. They are free to set their own hours, although some work evenings and weekends to accommodate patients' schedules. As entrepreneurs, there is room for creativity in structuring their work life.

The Profession

It is estimated that there are nearly ten thousand licensed acupuncture practitioners in the United States. This number is made up of two groups: physician and nonphysician acupuncturists. Although some physicians, dentists, and other practitioners elect to add acupuncture to their repertoire, it is not a common treatment method of M.D.s. Most licensed acupuncturists are nonphysicians—people who went to school to specifically study acupuncture.

In recent years the profession has received increasing support and acceptance. The World Health Organization (www.who.int), the American Osteopathic Association (www.osteopathic.org), the American Chiropractic Association (www.amerchiro.org), and the American Veterinary Medical Association (www.avma.org) all recognize and endorse acupuncture. More and more government funding has been appropriated for research, and increasing numbers of studies are being conducted.

In the past two decades, acupuncture has grown a great deal in popularity in the United States. According to the 2002 National Health Interview Survey—the largest and most comprehensive survey of complementary and alternative medicine (CAM) use by American adults to date—an estimated 8.2 million U.S. adults had used acupuncture, and an estimated 2.1 million U.S. adults had used acupuncture in the previous year. That is a lot of potential clients!

Training and Qualifications

Most people become acupuncturists because they have the desire to help other people. Success in this field requires belief in Chinese medicine philosophies, academic knowledge, technical skills, manual dexterity, sensitivity, and interpersonal skills. Knowledge of acupuncture techniques combined with a caring attitude are important qualities for this career.

Physician acupuncturists are allowed to practice acupuncture anywhere in the United States, and the licensing requirements are more lenient for M.D.s than for non-M.D.s. A few states only allow M.D.s to practice acupuncture. For physicians, the American Academy of Medical Acupuncture (www.medicalacupuncture.org) requires a minimum of two hundred hours of acupuncture training in addition to medical school training.

The majority of acupuncturists are nonphysician acupuncturists. Currently there are more than fifty schools of acupuncture in the United States. At least two years of college or a bachelor's degree with prerequisites such as biology, anatomy and physiology, psychology, and chemistry are required for acceptance into an acupuncture program. Programs award degrees leading to the titles of

Certified Acupuncturist (C.A.), Licensed Acupuncturist (Lic.Ac.), Diplomate in Acupuncture (Dipl.Ac.), and Master's or Doctor of Oriental Medicine (D.O.M.).

Training at recognized acupuncture schools takes from two to four years. A student of acupuncture takes approximately fifteen hundred to three thousand hours of courses and practical clinical internships. In the first and second years of study, students take courses such as Chinese medicine theory, diagnostic skills, counseling skills and ethics, Chinese language and medical terminology, clinical skills, herbal medicine, etiology and pathology of disease, Western pharmacology, and research design. Third and fourth years include a series of clinical internships and seminars and additional courses in Eastern and Western nutrition, advanced needle techniques, specialized approaches to theory and treatment, and practice management.

Licensing, certification, and regulation of acupuncturists vary from state to state. Currently thirty-five states and the District of Columbia license, certify, register, and officially recognize the practice of acupuncture. Twenty-four states and the District of Columbia license acupuncturists. Other states have different forms of regulation. A few states have no regulations. Many only allow medical doctors (M.D.s), doctors of osteopathy, and chiropractors to practice acupuncture, and some require acupuncturists to be supervised by a licensed physician.

Beyond licensure, the National Commission for Certification of Acupuncturists (NCCA; www.nccaom.org) certifies acupuncturists. This is particularly useful for acupuncturists in states that don't offer licensing. The NCCA requires a minimum of two years training at an accredited acupuncture school, or a four-year apprenticeship, and a written and practical exam.

Salary and Job Outlook

Acupuncture is definitely a growing field because more and more people hear about it and are open to alternatives. Insurance companies are also starting to cover things like acupuncture treatments, which will help increase exposure.

—Lisa Rothermich

The salary potential for acupuncturists varies greatly depending on the size of the practice, patients' ability to pay, geographic location, level of competition, and quality of service. Since most are self-employed, many acupuncturists treat patients as well as earn income from outside activities such as consulting, writing articles and books, conducting health education workshops, and teaching. A typical full-time salary can range between $25,000 and $50,000, although some can earn as much as $100,000 a year. Acupuncturists generally charge from $60 to $150 for a first appointment and $30 to $70 per follow-up visit. The overhead for starting a business is manageable because the cost of acupuncture equipment is relatively low.

The demand for acupuncture is growing with the number of people seeking acupuncture treatments increasing every year. Higher numbers of students are applying to acupuncture schools, and the acceptance of acupuncture by mainstream society and medicine is on the rise. Many insurance companies cover acupuncture, making it more accessible to patients.

Overall, the combination of acupuncture and traditional Chinese medicine is an excellent field to enter, providing you believe in the tenets or philosophy of the practice. If you're not sure whether this is the field for you, read more about this fascinating approach to health care before deciding against it. Even if, after further investigation, you decide not to enter this particular branch of holistic health, you'll find your knowledge base richer for the research you put into traditional Chinese medicine.

Professional Organizations

Accreditation Commission for Acupuncture and Oriental Medicine
www.acaom.org

American Academy of Medical Acupuncture
www.medicalacupuncture.org

American Association of Acupuncture and
    Oriental Medicine (AAOM)
www.aaom.org
(The nation's largest professional association organized to further the development of acupuncture as a complementary health care field.)

Council of Colleges of Acupuncture and Oriental Medicine
www.ccaom.org

National Acupuncture Foundation
www.nationalacupuncturefoundation.org

National Acupuncture and Oriental Medicine Alliance
www.acuall.org

National Certification Commission for Acupuncture and
    Oriental Medicine
www.nccaom.org
(Provides information about licensing laws by state and awards certification for acupuncturists.)

Schools

The following is a list of schools accredited by the Accreditation Commission for Acupuncture and Oriental Medicine.

Arizona

Arizona School of Acupuncture and Oriental Medicine
www.asaom.edu

Phoenix Institute of Herbal Medicine and Acupuncture
www.pihma.edu

California

Academy of Chinese Culture and Health Sciences
www.acchs.edu

Acupuncture and Integrative Medicine College–Berkeley
www.aimc.edu

American College of Traditional Chinese Medicine
www.actcm.edu

Dongguk Royal University
www.dru.edu

Emperor's College of Traditional Oriental Medicine
www.emperors.edu

Five Branches Institute: College of Traditional Chinese Medicine
www.fivebranches.edu

Samra University of Oriental Medicine
www.samra.edu

Santa Barbara College of Oriental Medicine
www.sbcom.edu

South Baylo University
www.southbaylo.edu

Southern California University of Health Sciences
www.scuhs.edu

University of East-West Medicine
www.uewm.edu

Yo San University of Traditional Chinese Medicine
www.yosan.edu

Colorado

Colorado School of Traditional Chinese Medicine
www.traditionalhealing.net

Southwest Acupuncture College
www.acupuncturecollege.edu

Florida

Academy for Five-Element Acupuncture
www.acupuncturist.com

Acupuncture and Massage College
www.amcollege.edu

Atlantic Institute of Oriental Medicine
www.atom.edu

Dragon Rises College of Oriental Medicine
www.dragonrises.net

East West College of Natural Medicine
www.ewcollege.org

Florida College of Integrative Medicine
www.fcim.edu

Hawaii

Institute of Clinical Acupuncture and Oriental Medicine
www.orientalmedschool.com

Traditional Chinese Medical College of Hawaii
www.tcmch.edu

World Medicine Institute: College of Acupuncture and
Oriental Medicine
www.acupuncture-hi.com

Illinois

Midwest College of Oriental Medicine
www.acupuncture.edu

Pacific College of Oriental Medicine
www.pacificcollege.edu

Maryland

Tai Sophia Institute
www.tai.edu

Massachusetts

New England School of Acupuncture
www.nesa.edu

Minnesota

American Academy of Acupuncture and Oriental Medicine
www.aaaom.org

Minnesota College of Acupuncture and Oriental Medicine
www.nwhealth.edu

New Jersey

Eastern School of Acupuncture and Traditional Medicine
www.easternschool.com

New York

Mercy College: Program in Acupuncture and Oriental Medicine
www.mercy.edu

New York College of Health Professions
www.nycollege.edu

New York College of Traditional Chinese Medicine
www.nyctcm.edu

Swedish Institute: School of Acupuncture and Oriental Studies
www.swedishinstitute.edu

Tri-State College of Acupuncture
www.tsca.edu

North Carolina

Jung Tao School of Classical Chinese Medicine
www.jungtao.edu

Oregon

National College of Naturopathic Medicine
www.ncnm.edu

Oregon College of Oriental Medicine
www.ocom.edu

Texas

Academy of Oriental Medicine at Austin
www.aoma.edu

American College of Acupuncture and Oriental Medicine
www.acaom.edu

Texas College of Traditional Chinese Medicine
www.texastcm.edu

Washington

Bastyr University
www.bastyr.edu

Seattle Institute of Oriental Medicine
www.siom.com

3

CHIROPRACTIC

CHIROPRACTIC IS A safe, nonsurgical, and drug-free approach to health care. Chiropractors use hands-on manipulation of the musculoskeletal system to enhance the body's own healing abilities and prevent disease. They focus on the relationship between the brain, spine, and the nervous system, together called the *central nervous system*. The musculoskeletal system and the central nervous system are interrelated, and problems in one area can cause dysfunction in the other. Communication between the brain, spine, and nervous system is essential for health, and interference in this communication is believed to cause health problems and their resulting symptoms. The goal of chiropractic care is to adjust the body and spine to remove interferences and bring the spine and central nervous system into alignment. This allows the body to heal and sustain health.

Philosophy

I am truly blessed and couldn't imagine doing anything else. I get to work with people and the product we sell is life and health. There are no gimmicks or gadgets, and what we are selling is life from within.

—Ann Ernish, Doctor of Chiropractic

The roots of chiropractic care can be traced back to the beginning of recorded time. Writings from ancient China and Greece (2700 B.C. and 1500 B.C., respectively) mention spinal manipulation and the maneuvering of the lower extremities to ease low back pain. Hippocrates, the famous Greek physician (460–357 B.C.) published texts detailing the importance of chiropractic care. In one of his writings he declares, "Obtain knowledge of the spine, for this is the requisite for many diseases."

In the United States, the practice of spinal manipulation began gaining momentum in the late nineteenth century when Dr. Daniel Palmer "officially" founded the practice of modern chiropractic care in 1895. Through his extensive study in anatomy and physiology, he proposed that there was an interrelationship between the musculoskeletal system and the central nervous system and that each relied on the other for health. Chiropractic philosophy holds that health depends on the normal functioning of the central nervous system—it is seen as the life force of the body. According to Palmer, every disease is at least partially affected by the nervous system's ability to flow freely, reach, and energize that area. Injury to the spinal nerves can result in problems in organs or tissues that are connected to those nerves. Injuries, misalignment, pressure, or compressions on the spinal nerve are called *subluxations*. Subluxations cut off nerve flow and affect bodily functions and cause symptoms. Chiropractors work to eliminate interference between the central nervous system and body joints and organs. By increasing freedom and flexibility in the spine, nerve flow is reestablished and symptoms can be improved or alleviated.

Chiropractors use a holistic, vitalistic philosophy that looks at the whole person in terms of life and health, rather than focusing on disease. They believe in the body's innate intelligence to heal and work to facilitate this intelligence, rather than treat disease directly. They recognize that a problem or symptom in one area of the body may be coming from another area of the body. Thus, chiropractors don't focus on a specific symptom of illness, but look at the underlying causes. Chiropractors also look at the whole person—body, mind, and spirit—to understand a patient's health. They acknowledge that physical, emotional, psychological, and social traumas or stressors can cause health problems, and they emphasize the use of natural, nondrug, nonsurgical alternatives to health care. Any illness can benefit from chiropractic care.

Types of Clients and Problems

This is confusing to consumers, who wonder why we are treating neck pain, ear infections, and asthma. What we really look at is the central nervous system, which is the brain and spinal cord.
—Ann Ernish

The greatest strength of chiropractic is in the treatment of low back pain, which has been supported by numerous research studies. Chiropractors are also well known for treating neuromuscular problems; head, neck, and arm problems; migraines; and knee, wrist, ankle, and other joint problems. Chiropractors do not prescribe medication, perform major surgery, or treat fractures or emergency trauma conditions.

Most people think chiropractors treat only neck and back pain, but they actually treat a wide array of health problems. Chiropractic treatment focuses on neuromusculoskeletal conditions and problems in the central nervous system. Problems in this system can result in a variety of health problems that may or may not appear to have to do with the spine. Chiropractors treat problems that are the result of injury, pressure, or misalignment of the spine. Since they work to treat the underlying causes of problems, they see patients with a wide variety of symptoms caused from central nervous system dysfunction. For example, chiropractors see patients with problems such as:

Neck/back pain	Lowered immune system
Ear infections	Colds
Asthma	Ulcers
Allergies	Respiratory problems
HIV/AIDS	Gynecological problems
Sports injuries	Mental/nervous disorders

Chiropractors can treat such a range of ailments because they work from the inside out by looking at the central nervous system for the cause of problems. When assessing a patient, if they don't find any type of dysfunction in the central nervous system, they may decide that the patient is not appropriate for chiropractic care. A patient may not have a misalignment of the spine even if he or she has neck pain. In these cases, chiropractors may provide counseling and make referrals.

Chiropractors work with all types of people, from infants to the elderly. The length of treatment varies from patient to patient, although treatment usually involves a series of visits. Some patients can be helped in one or two sessions, while others may need to go regularly for years.

Type of Care Rendered

As people become more educated and frustrated with the disease-care model of mainstream medicine, they are looking into other ways to protect their family. Chiropractic is a very viable option for families who don't want to pump medication into their children, but want to ensure good health.

—Ann Ernish

Chiropractors use many standard methods of diagnosing problems. They take x-rays, order blood work and laboratory tests, and conduct physical, neurological, and orthopedic exams. Their physical exams are similar to exams of traditional doctors. The initial visit plays an important role in diagnosing problems. Chiropractors take a detailed health history and description of symptoms. They also ask questions to assess other physical, emotional, and lifestyle factors that may influence health, including taking a thorough diet history. In addition, they complete an analysis of a patient's posture and spine.

The technique unique to chiropractic care is the use of chiropractic adjustments. *Chiropractic* is derived from Greek words meaning "done by hand." A chiropractic adjustment is when a doctor applies direct and controlled pressure to the spine and joints using his or her hands. Some adjustments are light reflex adjustments; others are deep concentrated adjustments to the spinal column. The goal of an adjustment is to remove subluxations; restore normal joint, nerve, and spine function; and increase mobility. Adjustments are not painful if done correctly.

In addition, chiropractors use supportive therapies to enhance the healing process and the benefits of chiropractic adjustments. Such additional techniques include: hot/cold compresses, hydrotherapy (use of hot/cold water), infrared and ultraviolet light, cranial manipulation, ultrasound, baths, electrical stimulation, traction, and heat therapy. Most chiropractors use various forms of massage therapy. These additional methods enhance the connection between the body's nerves and its organs and tissues. Other supportive measures include the use of heel or sole lifts, braces, straps, tapes, rehabilitative exercises, and physical therapy.

Chiropractors also provide general counseling to patients. They listen to their concerns and offer counseling on nutrition/dietary changes, sleep habits, personal hygiene, posture, work, and stress management. They support their patients in making changes to healthier lifestyles. They may suggest nutritional supplements, specific dietary regimens, or other activities that would enhance the body's natural ability to heal.

There are variations within the field of chiropractic. Most chiropractors are generalists who incorporate multiple healing methods into their care, including nutrition, homeopathy, massage, acupuncture, herbs and vitamins, and others. A second, smaller group of chiropractors do not use outside healing modalities and limit their care to chiropractic adjustments and spinal subluxations. These chiropractors refer to themselves as "straight" chiropractors. Finally, some chiropractors develop a specialty limiting their practice to specific health problems, and others work closely with allopathic (mainstream medical) physicians.

Employment Settings and Working Conditions

Once you graduate and have a license to practice, you can make your own hours. I see patients three days a week, for a total of about thirty hours, and then I put in another ten hours on paperwork and administrative tasks. This lifestyle enables you to have a lot of goals, and it provides you with quite a bit of flexibility in your personal life.

—Ann Ernish

The primary employment setting for chiropractors is individual or group private practice. Group practices are typically with other chiropractors, but some include other health practitioners. Chiropractors also have the option to conduct research, write articles or books, work at hospitals, or teach at colleges of chiropractic. Once licensed, chiropractors have the option to work in any capacity they desire.

As entrepreneurs, chiropractors have the flexibility to design their own work environment. They work in professional, comfortable settings and have the freedom to set their own hours. To meet the needs of patients, some choose to work evenings or weekends, but they typically work the traditional schedule of weekdays. A typical chiropractor in private practice works thirty-seven hours a week. Chiropractors also set their own goals for their practice. They decide their fee scales, finances, and how many patients to see each week.

Like any self-employed professional, chiropractors have the responsibility for running a business. In addition to seeing patients, chiropractors are responsible for marketing and advertising, billing patients and insurance companies, keeping records, and managing the office. Most chiropractors have office employees working for them and are responsible for supervising their staffs as well.

The Profession

The number of chiropractors in the United States is growing by leaps and bounds. According to government statistics, there are about fifty-five thousand chiropractors in the United States, a number that continues to rise every year. It is the second largest of the three primary health care providers in the nation—medicine, chiropractic, and osteopathy. Of the holistic health care providers, chiropractic is the largest profession. Chiropractors can be found practicing everywhere in the United States, from small towns to major cities, with all fifty states, the District of Columbia, Puerto Rico, and the Virgin Islands recognizing and regulating chiropractic. Chiropractic is also well known and respected throughout the world. It is available in sixty-two countries, and there are schools of chiropractic in Australia, New Zealand, South Africa, Great Britain, Denmark, and Japan. It is one of the most accepted holistic health care professions by the traditional medical system. Chiropractic care is available through Medicare and Medicaid and is covered by almost all insurance companies.

Training and Qualifications

In order to succeed in this field, you need to possess strong communication and problem-solving skills. If you have a passion and drive to contribute to the health of many people, and want to create a paradigm shift in health care, you'll make a very successful chiropractor.

—Ann Ernish

In 2005 the Council on Chiropractic Education accredited fifteen chiropractic programs and two chiropractic institutions in the United States. Applicants are required to have at least ninety semester hours of undergraduate study leading toward a bachelor's degree, including courses in English, the social sciences or humanities, organic and inorganic chemistry, biology, physics, and psychology. Many applicants have a bachelor's degree, which may eventually become the minimum entry requirement.

Chiropractic programs require a minimum of forty-two hundred hours (four to five years) of combined classroom, laboratory, and clinical experience, resulting in a Doctor of Chiropractic (D.C.) degree. During the first two years, most chiropractic programs emphasize classroom and laboratory work in basic science subjects such as anatomy, physiology, public health, microbiology, pathology, and biochemistry. In the third and fourth year, students gain clinical skills by working under the direct supervision of a chiropractor and learn to examine, diagnose, and adjust patients. Students gain practical training by working in college clinics or with selected chiropractors in private practice. In the final year, students receive training on business management and learn to set up practices, manage finances, and use advertising techniques.

Chiropractic colleges also offer postdoctoral training in orthopedics, neurology, sports injuries, nutrition, rehabilitation, radiology, industrial consulting, family practice, pediatrics, and applied chiropractic sciences. Once such training is complete, chiropractors may take specialty exams offered by associations for that area of specialty. Passing these exams leads to *diplomate* status in a given specialty.

Some chiropractors decide they want to specialize in certain areas of interest after receiving their degree. The American Chiropractic Association offers postgraduate certification programs leading to a diplomate status in areas such as orthopedics, nutrition, sports injuries, internal disorders, and radiology.

To be successful both in school and as a practicing chiropractor, students need strong manual skills, hand dexterity, the ability to work independently, attention to detail, time management skills, and the ability to handle a high level of responsibility. They must have a deep interest in helping sick people. And, as with all helping professions, empathy, understanding, patience, tact, adaptability, and emotional maturity are qualities needed to successfully work with patients.

Upon graduation from chiropractic school, chiropractors must pass national boards to obtain licensure. Most states recognize the exam administered by the National Board of Chiropractic Examiners (www.nbce.org), but some states require passing additional state exams. Requirements vary from state to state. Many states have reciprocal agreements, so once licensed it is easier for chiropractors to move from state to state. In addition, most states require continuing education to maintain licensure.

Salary and Job Outlook

In chiropractic, as in other types of independent practice, earnings are relatively low in the beginning and increase as the practice grows. Geographic location and the characteristics and qualifications of the practitioner also may influence earnings. Self-employed chiropractors must provide their own health insurance and retirement funds, so this will cut into overall earnings. According to government statistics, the median annual earnings of salaried chiropractors are about $70,000. The middle 50 percent of those working in the United States earn between $46,700 and $118,300 a year. According to another survey conducted by *Chiropractic Economics* magazine in 2005, the mean salary for chiropractors was $104,363.

Chiropractic is a growing field with excellent opportunities for new professionals. With new attitudes toward preventive health care and the high cost of medical treatments, both individuals and insurance companies are turning to chiropractic. Ten to fifteen percent of the population now use chiropractic, and virtually all health insurance companies cover the cost of chiropractic care. The growth of this field can be attributed to recent scientific research supporting the benefits of chiropractic care, patient testimonials, a growing public awareness of health care issues, and the demand by the public for medical alternatives. This is an excellent field to enter.

Professional Organizations

American Chiropractic Association
www.acatoday.org

Council on Chiropractic Education
www.cce-usa.org

International Chiropractic Association
www.chiropractic.org

World Chiropractic Alliance
www.worldchiropracticalliance.org

Licensing Information

Federation of Chiropractic Licensing Boards
www.fclb.org

National Board of Chiropractic Examiners
www.nbce.org

Schools

Cleveland Chiropractic College
www.clevelandchiropractic.edu

Life Chiropractic College
www.lifewest.edu

Logan College of Chiropractic
www.logan.edu

Los Angeles College of Chiropractic
www.scuhs.edu

National College of Chiropractic
www.national.chiropractic.edu

National University of Health Sciences
www.nuhs.edu

New York Chiropractic College
www.nycc.edu

Northwestern Health Sciences University
www.nwhealth.edu

Palmer College of Chiropractic
www.palmer.edu

Parker College of Chiropractic
www.parkercc.edu

Sherman College of Straight Chiropractic
www.sherman.edu

Texas Chiropractic College
www.txchiro.edu

University of Bridgeport
www.bridgeport.edu

Western States Chiropractic College
www.wschiro.edu

4

HOLISTIC DENTISTRY

HOLISTIC DENTISTS ARE traditionally trained and licensed dentists who incorporate holistic philosophy and alternative treatment methods into their dental practice. Holistic dentists work on the teeth and mouth like all dentists, but they are conscious that they are treating the whole person. The teeth are believed to be related to the whole body, and each tooth corresponds to specific organs and body parts via acupuncture meridians and energy pathways. Holistic dentists examine how teeth and gum problems can be affecting the overall health of a patient. They tend to practice conservative care by attempting to use the least-invasive methods of treatment and are concerned with how to prevent periodontal disease. They view gum surgery as a last resort. Many are mercury-free dentists, and others incorporate homeopathy and herbal medicine into their practices. There is wide variation from dentist to dentist as this is a new and developing specialty area.

Philosophy

Holistic dentists have a holistic view of health. They look at a person's general health and are concerned with early detection and prevention of tooth problems and disease. They believe in the body's natural healing abilities and will use the least toxic methods of care. Specific to holistic dentistry is the belief that each tooth is related to body organs through acupuncture meridians or pathways. This philosophy came from Chinese medicine and acupuncture. Holistic dentists believe the bacteria residing in tooth sockets under gums can cause infections both in the gums and in different parts of the body. Cases have been cited of patients who have recovered from seemingly unrelated physical illnesses after receiving holistic dental care. There is also the belief that bacteria and microorganisms under the gums are compromising people's immune systems by forcing the immune system to be constantly activated whether an infection is evident or not. An exhausted and weakened immune system can cause the body to be out of balance and can lead to illness. For this reason, many holistic dentists are concerned with controlling or eliminating bacteria with deep periodontal cleanings and irrigations.

Types of Clients and Problems

Most of the people who come into my office have alternative lifestyles and are into some form of alternative medicine. They are appreciative and grateful that I spend so much time with them. That is the nicest part about being a dentist.
—Bernard Schechter, Doctor of Dental Surgery

Since holistic dentists complete mainstream dental school and are licensed, they are qualified to provide full dental care and see patients with all types of dental problems. They provide typical care expected from any dentist, such as regular checkups, cleanings, fillings, crowns, tooth repair, and other typical dental health problems. It is the additional study they pursue and their own philosophy of holism that sets them apart from traditional dentists.

Clients who are knowledgeable about health and interested in receiving holistic care gravitate toward holistic dentists. In addition to the average client, holistic dentists may see clients who are receiving other forms of holistic care for health problems such as allergies, environmental illnesses, chronic fatigue syndrome, or health problems that are not responding to standard medicine. Some clients may seek holistic dentists as another avenue for treating their physical health problems. Others want to discuss how their diet is affecting their dental health, or they want their mercury fillings removed and replaced with a less-toxic material. Some clients who have been told they need gum surgery see holistic dentists to explore other options. Clients who want to avoid a root canal may seek out a holistic dentist to try more conservative methods for saving a tooth. Typically, clients are knowledgeable about holistic health care and their own physical, emotional, and spiritual condition.

Types of Treatment

It is more conservative dentistry. I try to save tooth structure and avoid surgery as much as possible. I want to give the body a chance to heal and give the immune system time to be activated, rather than going after things with a drill.

—Bernard Schechter

In addition to all the services provided by any dentist, holistic dentists offer different forms of treatment. One area that is common among holistic dentists is the elimination of the use of silver fillings. Standard silver fillings contain up to 50 percent elemental mercury. Studies have shown that mercury from tooth fillings can migrate and become deposited in other body organs, and this can lead to health problems. Many holistic dentists are "mercury free" and use less-toxic alternative substances for cavity fillings.

Another unique treatment in holistic dentistry is the use of homeopathy and herbal medicine. Homeopathy and herbal medicine are used to prevent gum disease and minimize pain, inflammation, infection, anxiety, stress, and fear in a patient. Typically these are used in conjunction with traditional dental medicine to aid in the healing process. A cavity can't be cured from homeopathy or herbal medicine, but these additional treatments can enhance healing and comfort for patients. Since holistic dentists are concerned with using the least-toxic methods possible, many try to avoid gum surgery and root canals. Again, gum surgery or root canals are necessary for many patients, but a holistic dentist will try other avenues of treatment before resorting to surgery. This can include herbal mouthwashes or deep periodontal cleanings under the gums with herbal solutions.

Many holistic dentists spend quite a bit of time counseling clients on diet and nutrition. They will discuss a client's diet and how it is impacting their dental health. They educate patients on the relationship between dental health and the body and often discuss current health issues. Some holistic dentists advocate the use of vitamin and mineral supplements. Supplements can be used to detoxify the body, supplement the diet for what is causing gums to be inflamed, or remineralize decaying teeth.

It is a broad field, with some dentists utilizing many alternative treatment methods and others offering only a few different approaches. Some holistic dentists focus on mercury-free fillings;

others focus on nutrition, herbal medicine, homeopathy, or specific problems such as TMJ (temporal mandibular joint) dysfunction. The common thread for all holistic dentists is the use of conservative dental care, where the body is given a chance to heal itself before resorting to severe measures.

Employment Settings and Working Conditions

Holistic dentists work in the same environments as traditional dentists working in individual or group private practices. Group practices are typically with other dentists, although some may include nutritionists or massage therapists. Their offices are clean and professional, and they include dental equipment and technology. A holistic dentist's office may have educational reading materials on homeopathy, herbalism, and other topics that would not be found in a traditional dentist's office, but overall the settings are similar. Dentists also have the option to conduct research, write articles, or teach at dental medical schools.

As entrepreneurs, holistic dentists have the flexibility to design their own work environment. They set their own goals for their practice and decide work schedules, fee scales, vacations, and how many patients to see each week. Holistic dentists typically have longer appointments and rarely see patients for less than one hour. It is common for the first fifteen to twenty minutes of an appointment to be spent talking with patients, learning about their overall physical condition, stress level, sensitivities, allergies, and concerns. Successful holistic dentists have patience and strong interpersonal skills.

Being a dentist is physically demanding. Dentists often have trouble with their eyesight as they get older because of the small area and instruments they work with. The work can also cause strain in the neck, back, hands, and elbows from bending over and using hands and arms for drilling. Dentists need to keep in shape and take care of their own physical health.

Like any self-employed professional, holistic dentists have the responsibility for running a business. In addition to seeing patients, they are responsible for marketing and advertising their services, billing patients and insurance companies, keeping records, and managing the office. Most holistic dentists have office employees working for them and are responsible for supervising their staff as well.

Training and Qualifications

First, go to dental school; then, get a license. When you're out in the real world, you can create your own type of holistic practice. Be prepared to do a lot of reading, studying, and pursuing continuing education in areas such as homeopathy, herbalism, craniosacral work, and other areas of the holistic movement.

—Bernard Schechter

To become a holistic dentist, one must first become a dentist by attending dental school and earning a license to practice. All states require dentists to become licensed. Dental school typically takes four years to complete. Admission to dental school requires at least two years of college-level predental education in the sciences, although most applicants have a bachelor's degree when entering dental school. Dental schools award the degree of Doctor of Dental Surgery (D.D.S.) or Doctor of Dental Medicine (D.M.D.). After obtaining your degree, most states will require you to pass written and practical exams. Once licensed, you will then be free to design your own practice, and this is where holistic dental training begins.

To become a holistic dentist, additional training in the holistic philosophy and alternative treatments is required. Obtaining training is flexible and there are no set standards or minimum requirements. There are no dental schools that teach holistic dentistry, so it is up to the dentist to take the initiative to receive training and develop a specialty in holistic dentistry.

Training can take many forms. The best way for a dentist to learn about holistic dentistry is to join one of the holistic dental professional associations. The Holistic Dental Association (www .holisticdental.org), the Dental Health Foundation (www.dental healthfoundation.org), and the International Academy of Oral Medicine and Toxicology (www.iaomt.org) are dental organizations concerned with holistic dentistry. They offer meetings, conferences, and seminars for dentists to receive training on new techniques. They also publish newsletters and literature so concerned dentists can participate in and learn more about different perspectives and attitudes of holistic dentistry.

In addition to joining and participating in holistic dental organizations, dentists can also develop their specialty through self-study in other areas of holistic care. Some holistic dentists take classes or seminars on nutrition, herbalism, or other holistic modalities to complement their training. This knowledge is helpful because many clients who seek holistic dentists are involved in other areas of holistic health care as well. For many dentists, becoming a holistic dentist is an ongoing learning process that continues throughout their careers.

Salary and Job Outlook

Expect that the income might not be as high as a regular general practitioner who doesn't have a consciousness of holistic health, because you will have to give more time to conversation and interaction than does a mechanical dentist. You can still do very well; it's just more difficult to mass produce.

—Bernard Schechter

According to government statistics, the median annual earnings of salaried dentists were $129,920 in May 2004. Earnings vary according to the number of years in practice, location, hours worked, and specialty. Self-employed dentists in private practice tend to earn more than do salaried dentists. Like other business owners, self-employed dentists must provide their own health insurance, life insurance, and retirement benefits.

Holistic dentists can expect to earn similar, although slightly lower salaries than mainstream dentists. Holistic dentists may have different rate/pay scales because they tend to spend more time with patients in long appointments. They may need to charge more per office visit to balance out their long appointments and retain a competitive salary.

The field of holistic dentistry is a small but growing specialty area in dental medicine. The employment prospects for dentists as a whole are expected to have fairly good, although not outstanding, job growth. Most of the growth will come from the need to replace older retiring dentists. Although the demand for dental care will be high due to needed care for children and the elderly, dental hygienists and assistants will also be available to meet the demands. Though there are no data to predict the demand for holistic dentists specifically, as the field of holistic health care grows it will likely increase the demand for holistic dentists. As our society becomes interested in preventive health and alternative care methods, people will become aware of these options for dental health as well.

Professional Organizations

American Dental Association
www.ada.org

American Dental Education Association
www.adea.org

Dental Health Foundation
www.dentalhealthfoundation.org

Holistic Dental Association
www.holisticdental.org

International Academy of Oral Medicine and Toxicology
www.iaomt.org

Licensing Information

American Dental Association Council on Dental Education and
Licensure
www.ada.org

American Association of Dental Examiners
www.aadexam.org

Schools

The following are dental schools accredited by the American Dental Association.

Alabama

University of Alabama
www.dental.uab.edu

Arizona

A.T. Still University of Health Sciences
www.ashs.edu/dental

California

Loma Linda University
www.llu.edu/llu/dentistry

University of California–Los Angeles
www.dent.ucla.edu

University of California–San Francisco
www.ucsf.edu

University of Southern California
www.usc.edu/hsc/dental

University of the Pacific
http://dental.pacific.edu

Colorado

University of Colorado
www.uchsc.edu/sod

Connecticut

University of Connecticut
http://sdm.uchc.edu

District of Columbia

Howard University
www.howard.edu

Florida

Nova Southeastern University
http://dental.nova.edu

University of Florida
www.dental.ufl.edu

Georgia

Medical College of Georgia
www.mcg.edu/sod

Illinois

Southern Illinois University
www.siue.edu/sdm

University of Illinois
http://dentistry.uic.edu

Indiana

Indiana University
www.iusd.iupui.edu

Iowa

University of Iowa
www.dentistry.uiowa.edu

Kentucky

University of Kentucky
www.mc.uky.edu/dentistry

University of Louisville
www.dental.louisville.edu/dental

Louisiana

Louisiana State University
www.lsusd.lsuhsc.edu

Maryland

University of Maryland
www.dental.umaryland.edu

Massachusetts

Boston University
http://dentalschool.bu.edu

Harvard University
www.hsdm.med.harvard.edu

Tufts University
www.tufts.edu/dental

Michigan

University of Michigan
www.dent.umich.edu

University of Detroit Mercy
www.udmercy.edu/dental

Minnesota

University of Minnesota
www.dentistry.umn.edu

Mississippi

University of Mississippi
http://dentistry.umc.edu

Missouri

University of Missouri
www.umkc.edu/dentistry

Nebraska

University of Nebraska Medical Center
www.unmc.edu/dentistry

Creighton University
http://cudental.creighton.edu

Nevada

University of Nevada
http://dentalschool.unlv.edu

New Jersey

University of Medicine and Dentistry of New Jersey
www.umdnj.edu

New York

Columbia University
http://cpmcnet.columbia.edu/dept/dental

New York University
www.nyu.edu/dental

State University of New York–Buffalo
www.sdm.buffalo.edu

State University of New York–Stonybrook
www.hsc.stonybrook.edu/dental

North Carolina

University of North Carolina
www.dent.unc.edu

Ohio

Case Western Reserve University
www.case.edu/dental/site/main.html

Ohio State University
www.dent.ohio-state.edu

Oklahoma

University of Oklahoma
http://dentistry.ouhsc.edu

Oregon

Oregon Health and Science University
www.ohsu.edu/sod/admissions

Pennsylvania

Temple University
www.temple.edu/dentistry

University of Pennsylvania
www.dental.upenn.edu

University of Pittsburgh
www.dental.pitt.edu

Puerto Rico

University of Puerto Rico
http://dental.rcm.upr.edu

South Carolina

Medical University of South Carolina College
www.gradstudies.musc.edu/dentistry/dental.html

Tennessee

University of Tennessee
www.utmem.edu/dentistry

Meharry Medical College
http://dentistry.mmc.edu

Texas

Baylor College
www.tambcd.edu

University of Texas
www.dental.uthscsa.edu

Virginia

Virginia Commonwealth University
www.dentistry.vcu.edu

Washington

University of Washington
www.dental.washington.edu

West Virginia

West Virginia University School of Dentistry
www.hsc.wvu.edu/sod

Wisconsin

Marquette University School of Dentistry
www.dental.mu.edu

5

Energy Healing

ACCORDING TO ANCIENT Japanese, Chinese, and Indian traditions, every human has an energy field around him or her called an *aura*, *euphoric body*, *energy field*, or *electromagnetic field*. Energy healers use their energy and the energy fields of clients to heal physical and psychological problems. Energy healers are guided by a spiritual higher intelligence and direct or change energy where it is needed in a client. The process involves various hand positions and movements to influence the flow of energy. It is a noninvasive and completely benign technique for healing the mind and the body.

Energy healing is a broad term that refers to any approach that uses an awareness of the energy field for healing. This chapter discusses energy healing in general and covers common types of energy healing such as Reiki, therapeutic touch, and polarity. Keep an open mind while reading, and research the areas covered on your own. You might discover that not only is there an abundance of practitioners of energy healing, but there is an even greater number of believers testifying to the effects of this unique form of holistic health care.

Philosophy

There is energy in everything. You have probably noticed that when you are with someone who is stressed out and their energy is high, you might feel agitated being around them. That's because our energy fields are interacting all the time.

—Leslie Newman, Holistic Psychotherapist
and Energy Healer

The philosophy of energy healing is based on the belief that energy fields exist in all living things, including plants, animals, and humans. Health comes from clear and free-flowing energy throughout the body. The body's energy is affected by food, air, sleep, thoughts, and emotions. When a person's energy is clear and flowing, the body and the mind are healthy. When the energy is low, blocked, or disrupted, the physical organs and tissues will be adversely affected. Negative thoughts and feelings play a strong role in the flow of one's energy and overall health.

From this philosophy, the mind and body are seen as one. Energy healers believe the mind exists not only in the brain, but throughout the whole body. The mind extends to every part of the body through the central nervous system, circulatory system, and endocrine system. The brain is constantly sending and receiving messages to and from the body, creating the mind/body connection. This connection explains the influence of thoughts and feelings on physical health. Energy healers also believe that mind/body energy exists in a subtle energy field extending approximately two to three feet outside the body. This field surrounding the body is often referred to as the *aura*. Negative thoughts collect and disturb energy in the aura and in locations throughout the body. The physical organs existing in these locations are hampered by the restriction of energy flow, and illness results.

Finally, many energy healers believe that a higher power, higher intelligence, or God guides the functioning of the universe. Energy healers often use a sense of spiritual guidance to help them in their work with clients. From this perspective, the energy flow is guided by a higher power and can work on the unconscious parts of the mind/body that are inhibiting energy flow.

Types of Clients and Problems

The nature of diseases has changed from the 1950s with debilitating diseases like polio responding well to drugs. Now there are so many more stress-related and chronic diseases such as heart disease and fibromyalgia. Energy healing in conjunction with the medical profession can help treat those who are suffering from such ailments.

—Leslie Newman

Energy healing focuses on improving a client's energy flow, as opposed to treating any specific symptoms or diseases. Thus, people with a wide range of physical and psychological problems seek energy healing. Energy healers often see clients who have physical problems that are not associated with a particular disease. They treat clients with fatigue, digestive problems, headaches, body aches, insomnia, frequent colds and flu, stress-related problems, and chronic fatigue syndrome. Many people who haven't been helped by mainstream medicine turn to energy healers as an alternative. Clients also include healthy people who are seeking more energy or want to prevent illness by clearing their energy fields. Finally, people with serious health problems such as cancer, AIDS, and heart disease seek energy healing as a complement to traditional medical treatment. Energy healing is used to enhance the healing process, reduce pain, and minimize side effects of medical intervention. Since energy healing is focused on clearing the energy fields rather than curing one symptom, it can help clients with any health problems.

Energy healers treat problems of the mind and body and see clients with a wide variety of psychological complaints such as anxiety, stress, irritability, and depression. Many times, blocked or low energy can manifest as a psychological problem; vice versa, a psychological problem can create low energy and physical health problems. Although they are not trained therapists, energy healers explore these issues because of the connection between mind, body, and energy field. Often when an energy healer is working with a client, emotions are released. Together the client and healer can explore how these emotions might be affecting the client's overall health.

Energy healing is appropriate for men and women of all ages, although more women than men tend to seek energy healing. It is not necessary for clients to understand or believe in energy healing philosophies to receive benefits of this therapy. However, many people who seek energy healing have some knowledge about and interest in mind/body principles.

Types of Care Rendered

I perceive energy through my five physical senses and through my expanded high sensory perception. I begin by aligning my intention with the good, the light, the divine, and I connect with the client's energy field. If we are working on the table, I can have my hands on the client or just over the body. Some clients are relaxed and almost asleep, and others can be very interactive.

—Leslie Newman

Energy healers have their own techniques for working with clients, but they all focus on using energy to heal. Typically, energy healers will spend the beginning of a first session talking with a client about current health problems, lifestyle, stress, and reason for seeking help. After discussion, the client can remain sitting or lie down, fully clothed, on a comfortable table. Energy healers start by grounding and centering themselves to clear their minds of personal thoughts. Many healers try to connect to a spiritual essence of universal energy. Energy healers do not use their own energy to heal because it would be too draining. Thus, they rely on channeling energy from a higher power, spiritual essence, universal energy, or God.

Energy healers develop high sensory perception to assess their client's energy fields. They look for blockages or disturbed energy fields and transmit clear and calming energy through placing their hands in certain positions along the body. Practitioners may place their hands on certain points of the body, or they may hold their hands a few inches away from the client. There is no pressure applied to a client, and healers use their hands to transfer energy from the universal energy field to a client's problem areas. A typical session lasts one hour. The length of treatment varies, depending on need. Most people find these sessions deeply relaxing.

Similar to acupuncture, energy healers believe there are points on the body, called *chakras,* that act as channels for the universal energy to flow in and out. Chakras are energy centers that run along the spine, and each chakra corresponds to different emotional states. A typical form of energy healing is to use a sequence of hand positions starting at the top of a client's head and working down the body along these points. There are seven chakras running along the spine. The first is at its base and is associated with governing the physical body and health. The second is located in the womb area and governs creativity and emotions. The third is located at the solar plexus and is associated with will and desire. The fourth is the heart chakra, which is connected to emotion and human love. The fifth is at the throat and influences communication. The sixth is in the mid-forehead and is connected with thought, vision, and spiritual love. The seventh is at the crown of the head and opens up to the divine or God. It is common for energy healers to focus on these energy points during treatments, although this is only one approach to working with a client's energy field.

Forms of Energy Healing

Energy healing is really broad. There are different schools of thought in energy healing, just like there are different schools of thought in psychology. I define energy healing as using the aware-ness of the energy field to help people with their physical and psy-chological issues.

—Leslie Newman

It should be noted that energy healing is typically not a substitute for appropriate medical care or psychotherapy. It is often used as an adjunct to other forms of medical care or to treat problems that have not been helped by other methods. Most clients of energy healers also see traditional medical doctors for treatment of their ailments.

Reiki

One of the most popular forms of energy healing in the United States is Reiki, which is a Japanese technique for stress reduction and relaxation that also promotes healing. The word *Reiki* comes from two Japanese words, *rei* and *ki*. *Rei* refers to the higher intelligence or power that guides the universe. *Ki* refers to the energy fields that exist in all living things. Thus, Reiki treats the whole person: the body, emotions, mind, and spirit. Reiki practitioners channel spiritual energy to heal physical, spiritual, and psychological problems. There is no use of massage or pressure; Reiki practitioners place their hands in certain positions on or above the body to transmit spiritual energy to the client. Clients report many beneficial effects including relaxation and feelings of peace, security, and well-being.

Therapeutic Touch

Therapeutic touch is an energy healing technique that was developed by Dr. Dolores Krieger, R.N., and Dora Kunz, a healer and Dr. Krieger's friend, in 1972 and is especially popular with those in the nursing profession. Therapeutic touch is an individualized intervention guided by cues gained from assessing an individual's energy field. Similar to other forms of energy healing, practitioners place their hands two to six inches above a client's body and transmit or manipulate the energy field to help heal specific health problems. Practitioners pass their hands over the body from head to toe in broad sweeping motions. Nurses use therapeutic touch to relieve stress and pain and to increase the healing process. It is composed of the following four steps.

Centering

Centering involves bringing the body, mind, and emotions to a focused state of consciousness. This is accomplished by using breath work, imagery, and meditation.

Assessing

During assessment, the nurse holds his or her hands two to six inches away from the client's energy field while moving the hands from the head to the feet in a rhythmical, symmetrical manner. Sensory cues such as warmth, coolness, static, blockage, pulling, and tingling are described by some practitioners.

Intervention

The intervention stage involves facilitating the symmetrical flow of energy through the client's energy field. Treatment is accomplished by moving the hands to the areas that seem to need attention; energy may be transferred where there is a deficit, or energy may be mobilized or moved from areas of congestion to areas where there is a lack of energy.

Evaluation/Closure

During the final stage, nurses use professional, informed, and intuitive judgment to determine when to end the session. They are constantly reassessing the client's energy field during the course of treatment to determine when energy balance is sufficient to end treatment.

Polarity

Polarity therapy is a form of energy healing d[...]
dolph Stone, a chiropractor, osteopathic phys[...]
Polarity is based on the belief that mental, p[...]
conditions are reflected in one's energy field. Polarity's go[...]
stimulate and balance the energy field to heal health problems. A
polarity therapist works with clients to address energy blockages
and may use bodywork, exercise, diet, and self-awareness exercises
to promote health.

Polarity therapy is different from the other energy healing methods because it does not have a spiritual focus. Polarity has a scientific view that the body is a source of both positive and negative energy resulting in energy currents and pulses running throughout it. When the positive and negative flow of energy is unbalanced, health problems can occur. In working with a client, a polarity therapist may use light touch, deep pressure, or rocking motions to balance a client's energy. The act of manipulating and balancing the energy is seen as the source of healing.

Employment Settings and Working Conditions

> *I know some hospitals give patients the option to have fifteen minutes of Reiki therapy before going into surgery. I have worked with people postoperatively, and energy healing works well with minimizing side effects and speeding up the healing process.*
> —Leslie Newman

Most energy healers are in a private or group practice where they see clients individually for consultations. They work in professional,

, comfortable offices or have offices out of their homes. The rk setting is typically a relaxed, quiet environment that is spacious enough to hold a padded table.

Energy healers can be found working with other holistic care practitioners such as acupuncturists, naturopaths, and massage therapists. Some energy healers are trained in a number of healing modalities and combine their training to use energy healing along with psychotherapy or massage therapy. Since energy healing can be used for any health problem, other health care providers incorporate it into their work.

As entrepreneurs, energy healers have the responsibility for running their businesses. Their success depends greatly on their ability to advertise and market their services. They also handle all financial aspects including billing, record keeping, and taxes.

Being self-employed allows energy healers the freedom to organize their schedules. They create their own hours and have control over how many clients they wish to see each week. Although they create their own schedules, they also must meet the needs of their clients, so some energy healers work evening or weekend hours.

Energy healers also find other settings and avenues for their work. Some make additional income by teaching at energy healing schools or by offering apprenticeships to aspiring energy healers. Some offer workshops or group sessions for additional income and marketing. A small number can be found working in hospitals or clinics as an adjunct to mainstream medicine.

The Profession

Energy healing is currently unregulated and there are no licensing or national requirements. Some states have regulations, but there is much confusion on how to regulate this occupation. In some states it is considered massage therapy, and massage therapy guidelines are followed. Other states have no guidelines. This means anyone can open an energy healing practice and call himself or herself an energy healer. This creates pros and cons for the field. On the positive side, it is easy for practitioners to open a practice, and there is great flexibility and creativity in the work. The difficulty is in setting baseline standards for the profession, and without licensure, energy healing will have a harder time gaining credibility. Currently the existing professional organizations provide the best guidelines for certification, adequate training, and practice standards.

Training and Qualifications

It is a unique path to becoming a healer. Just as there is a healer for everybody, I think there is a school for everybody. My path was to go to many different schools; the key is to know yourself and what works for you. Think about it holistically and look at the triangle of mind/body/spirit. See what you need to develop, and find a school that offers it.

—Leslie Newman

Training in energy healing varies greatly depending on individual interests and specialty areas. There are many different schools and training programs on each of the energy healing modalities: Reiki, polarity, and therapeutic touch. Training can range from a two-day Reiki training workshop to years of study. Many of the training programs for energy healing are nontraditional, with courses offered over several weeks, weekend training, summer sessions, and apprenticeships. Many require home study or correspondence courses in addition to training sessions and practical experience. Accreditation and certification vary from program to program. For example, the

American Polarity Therapy Association (www.polaritytherapy.org) accredits training schools that require at least 155 hours of training and meet its standards for practice. It is recommended that individuals interested in energy healing training contact professional associations in their area of interest for more information.

There are several areas of knowledge important for energy healers to learn and to look for in programs. One is grounding in anatomy and physiology. It is important to learn where things are in the body, so the connection between the energy points and the physical organs can be made. In addition, a background in psychology is helpful since energy healing can trigger emotional releases in clients. Learning basic counseling skills will help in working with clients. Specific training on energy fields and energy healing techniques is essential to gain an understanding of the intellectual, physical, spiritual, and emotional aspects of energy.

In addition to training, many energy healers find it helpful to maintain their own physical, emotional, and spiritual health. Since energy healers transfer energy through their own energy fields, it is helpful if their fields are free from toxins and negative energy to reduce transferring them to clients. A healthy diet, yoga, meditation, and other activities can help an energy healer maintain a healthy energy field.

Salary and Job Outlook

It is difficult to assess the job outlook and salary for these occupations because they are still fairly modest in terms of numbers of practitioners and clientele and because there are no credentialing or other standards that require tracking. It appears these fields are growing as they are organizing into professional associations and making their way into mainstream medical settings. Customer demand will likely continue to drive the growth of these occupations as more people seek alternatives to mainstream health care.

Salary depends on the ability of the practitioner to market his or her services and on the ability of the client to pay. Typically, energy healing is not covered by medical insurance, so clients pay out of pocket for services. Practitioners can charge anywhere from $40 to $70 per session, and many sessions last from one to two hours, depending on their background, training, and the market for their services. Some geographic areas will have more demand for holistic services than others, in particular urban settings, so practitioners should consider geography when opening a practice.

Professional Associations and Training Institutions

You will need to conduct considerable research into the quality of instruction offered by programs and institutions in the energy healing area. Because of this, we are including only a few of the more well-known organizations.

Reiki

American Reiki Master Association
www.atlantic.net/~arma

International Association of Reiki Professionals
www.iarp.org

International Center for Reiki Training
www.reiki.org

Reiki Alliance
www.reikialliance.com

ɪr Healing Arts

ɪrown.com

Connection

www.reikienergy.com

Therapeutic Touch

Barbara Brennan School of Healing
www.barbarabrennan.com

Healing Touch International
www.healingtouchinternational.org

Nurse Healers Professional Associates International
www.therapeutic-touch.org

Polarity

American Polarity Therapy Association
www.polaritytherapy.org

Polarity Healing Arts of Santa Monica
www.polarityhealingarts.com

Other

Association for Comprehensive Energy Psychology
http://energypsych.org

International Foundation of Bio-Magnetics
www.justtouch.com

International Society for the Study of Subtle Energy and Energy
Medicine
www.issseem.org

6

HERBALISM

HERBALISM OR HERBAL medicine is an ancient form of healing that uses plants and plant-based substances to treat illnesses and boost overall health. It is a plant science that involves identifying, harvesting, and developing the plant into forms for medicinal use. Each plant or herb has different chemical constituents with unique health benefits. For example, the herb ginger is known for its calming effect on the digestive system and is taken for upset stomachs and motion sickness. Valerian is a plant known for its ability to relax the mind and body and can relieve insomnia, anxiety, and tension headaches. It is no surprise that many prescription drugs sold in the United States are derived from plants.

The healing power of plants is well established worldwide, and herbalists use plants to contribute to overall wellness. Herbalism has been used for centuries all over the world, most extensively in Chinese medicine. In the United States, herbalism developed out of Eastern influence and family home remedies.

Philosophy

Herbalist philosophy is based on respect for the earth. Plants and herbs are seen as valuable gifts and are honored for their medicinal uses. They are also seen as beneficial food sources for sustaining the body. Many herbs are believed to support the immune system and the natural functioning of the body. While specific plants are used for specific ailments, herbalists use herbs to increase the body's own natural healing abilities. Herbalists are concerned with the whole person and use herbs to help alleviate physical, emotional, mental, and spiritual problems.

Types of Clients and Problems

There are hundreds of herbs on the planet that can be used for different health problems, so herbalists invariably see people with a wide range of health issues. They see clients of all ages, with both simple and serious health conditions. Their goal is to educate clients on the use of herbs to enhance overall well-being. They do not claim to cure specific problems but use herbs to boost the immune system, alleviate symptoms, and support overall health. Thus, herbalists can work with clients with any health problem.

Many people seek herbalists to prevent illness, increase energy, and maintain health. Although herbalists can't claim to cure problems, they can suggest herbs to assist with any health goal. Some of the more common health issues herbalists address include:

Sinus infections	Colds/flu
Digestive problems	Headaches
Fatigue	Hormone imbalances
Stress	Pregnancy

Insomnia	Menopause
Cancer	HIV/AIDS
Chronic conditions	Anxiety

Many people for whom traditional medicine has failed turn to herbalists for help. Some people want to try herbs as a first option to avoid traditional medicine or prescription drugs. Others use a combination of traditional medicine and herbalism. People with serious health problems such as cancer, heart disease, or AIDS/HIV, or people requiring surgery see herbalists along with other practitioners. They use herbalism as a way to support their body as they struggle with their particular disease and treatment. Herbalists can work with a wide range of clients because of their focus on overall health.

Types of Treatment

Providing education is the primary aspect of my job because I want people to know that this is service they can provide for themselves. I offer workshops and individual consultations and make my own products from a combination of growing and buying herbs.

—Rebecca Petee, Herbalist

Education, consultation, support, and herbal products make up the foundations of herbal care. Individual care is provided through one-on-one consultations. During an initial one-hour appointment, herbalists ask questions to assess their clients' needs and goals. Herbalists ask questions related to health history, symptoms of the presenting problem, reason for seeking help, diet, lifestyle, work, stress level, support system, sleep patterns, and the use of nutritional or other supplements. They look at the whole person when deciding on a plan for incorporating herbs into his or her life. They do not diagnose health problems but assess the client's health and potential benefits from using herbs.

Based on the assessment process, an herbalist will work with the client to develop a care plan. Herbalists are not doctors and therefore do not prescribe treatment. Much of an herbalist's job is to educate clients on the historical and demonstrated medicinal benefits of herbs. They teach clients about herbs and their specific health benefits, and they show clients how to incorporate herbs into their lives. From research they identify herbs that can meet the needs of a client's health problem or goal. Similar to other holistic health practitioners, herbalists encourage clients to take ownership and control over their own health. They hope to teach clients to use herbs as one tool for self-care.

Once specific herbs have been identified to meet specific client needs, herbalists offer the remedies in a variety of ways. An herbalist may make simple recommendations that a client eat more of a certain herb, such as garlic for increased immunity, or suggest that certain herbs be purchased at health food stores. Typically, herbalists make their own herbal remedies and make these available to clients. Herbalists may have their own stock of individual herbs or herbal combinations to be used by clients, or they develop a combination of herbs specific to a client's needs.

Herbal remedies take the form of teas or infusions, capsules, tinctures, infused oils, or salves. The form of herbal product suggested depends on personal preference, client preference, or the herbs being used. Herbal teas and infusions are simply made from the flowers, leaves, seeds, roots, and bark of fresh or dried herbs.

Capsules are made from finely grinding these parts of the plant and putting them into capsules. Herbalists make tinctures by steeping dried herbs in alcohol. All of these forms are used for consumption by the clients. Herbalists also make infused oils and salves for the use of herbs topically. Infused oils can be used for direct application or massage and are made from placing an herb in oil and letting it sit for a few weeks in the sun. Similarly, herbal salves are made from adding the herbal oil to beeswax. All forms offer the medicinal properties of the plant. The specific herbs and form the herbalist decides to use depend on the herbalist's style and the individual needs of the client. Techniques and remedies may vary, but all herbalists use the healing properties of plants to care for clients. Aromatherapy and flower essences are two specialty areas in the field of herbal medicine.

Aromatherapy

Aromatherapy is the art of using oils extracted from aromatic plants to enhance physical and emotional health. These oils are extracted from plants, flowers, herbs, spices, woods, and fibers usually by distillation or expression extraction. The essential oils are considered the life force of the plant and give the plant its scent. It is the scent of the plant that provides health benefits, and aromatherapy uses these scents to improve health. Herbalists who use aromatherapy suggest different methods of use. The oils are used in baths, compresses, and vaporizers. Often oils are included in massage oils to add the additional benefit of aromatherapy to massage. Oils can be inhaled directly from their containers or can be added to a bowl of steaming water. Finally, natural perfumes are made by blending different oils. Essential oils are used individually or in combination to aid with health problems. Many aromatherapy oils are made from common household spices. For example cinnamon, lemon, and clove are strong antiseptics. Lavender and jasmine are soothing and calming oils useful for stress, anxiety, and fatigue. As with herbs, there are many different essential oils, and how an herbalist incorporates these into care varies from practitioner to practitioner.

Flower Essences

Flower essences are an ancient technique of applying plant energy to health. This technique is experiencing a revival in popularity. Flower essences are created by placing flower petals in water and allowing them to sit in the sun for at least four hours. The specific healing energy of the flower is released into the water in a concentrated form. The water tincture is preserved in brandy, vinegar, or vegetable glycerin, and the liquid is taken orally a few drops at a time. The liquid does not have an aroma or color. The essences are believed to be imprinted with the life force energy of the plant and help balance physical, emotional, mental, and spiritual disharmony.

Employment Settings and Working Conditions

Herbalists work in private practice, run shops, sell their products, and work in companies manufacturing herbal products. Most have their own practice, teach workshops, or offer certificate programs.

—Rebecca Petee

There is a broad range of employment options available to herbalists, and the work conditions vary considerably. Typically, herbalists are self-employed in private practice. An herbalist in private practice sees clients individually for consultations in an office or home setting. In addition to consulting with clients, herbalists teach workshops on herbal topics at a variety of locales. Herbalists can be found teaching workshops at hospitals, health clinics, bookstores, libraries, community adult education programs, schools, private industry, and anywhere else on request. They teach workshops for people who want to learn to use herbs and for other health practitioners who want to add herbs to their work. Herbalists teach a variety of workshops to meet specific individual needs of groups. For example, an herbalist may teach a group of pregnant women about the use of herbs during pregnancy, or he or she may go into an elementary school and teach teachers the use of aromatherapy for calming hyperactive children in crowded classrooms. Herbs can be applied to many areas, and an herbalist in private practice develops workshops for different populations.

Another way for an herbalist to earn a living is in the creation of herbal products. As mentioned earlier, many herbalists make their own teas, tinctures, oils, and capsules to sell to individual clients or health food stores. Some herbalists open their own shops for selling their herbal products or expand into herbal beauty products and make natural soaps, lotions, shampoos, and bath products.

Herbalists can also be found working on staff with other health practitioners such as naturopathic physicians, chiropractors, and massage therapists. A few find work at hospitals or clinics. These opportunities may increase as holistic health care becomes more accepted by mainstream medicine.

Research and herbal manufacturing is another career option for herbalists. Herbalists can be found in the field studying plants all over the world or conducting research for herbal product compa-

nies. Companies that make herbal or natural products hire herbalists on staff or as consultants to advise them on products. Some
herbalists focus their career on herbal farming: the planting, growing, harvesting, and distributing of herbs wholesale to other herbalists. This in itself is a full-time job.

Finally, herbal education is an option for herbalists. Most of
herbal education is the completion of hands-on apprenticeship.
Once an herbalist has established a business and reputation, he or
she can design a program, set fees, and offer herbal apprenticeship
and training for new herbalists as another income source. While
apprenticeships are more common, some herbalists find work teaching at herbal schools.

As with any self-employed professional, herbalists have the
responsibility for running their businesses. This includes advertising, marketing, billing, and financial record keeping. Because they
are self-employed, herbalists have the freedom to set their own
schedules and work styles. The profession affords a lot of flexibility, creativity, and independence.

The Profession

The field of herbal medicine is currently developing in the United
States. It is not regulated and there are no licensing or standardized
guidelines for becoming an herbalist. The federal government is
starting to research certain herbs, and thereby the profession, but
no regulations have yet come from this. Some states and local communities have laws regulating herbalists, but for the most part anyone can start an herbal practice or business. Some states have banned
the use of certain herbs deemed dangerous, but this has been specific to certain herbs and not the profession. As the field continues

to grow, regulations may come into place to standardize it, but for now it is open to herbalists with various types of training.

One of the challenges for the field is to present the profession as legitimate and professional. In some parts of the United States, herbalism and holistic health are viewed with skepticism. Herbalists need to stay current with legal and scientific research in the field and must demonstrate their legitimacy. One problem herbalism has is the lack of hard scientific study. Herbs have been used for centuries in healing, but in the United States there has not been extensive scientific research. Studies and research demonstrating the effectiveness of herbs have been increasing and are likely to continue.

Training and Qualifications

My program was with Rosemary Gladstar, who has been an herbalist for more than twenty years. Her training was self-taught and came from knowledge passed down to her from her grandmother and mother. The program she offered consisted of one weekend a month for eight months. In addition, I completed a correspondence course. The fact is that every school is different; you just have to find one that works for you.

—Rebecca Petee

With little regulation of this profession, there is no one standard way to become an herbalist. Herbalists gain their knowledge and come to this profession through a variety of paths and backgrounds. It is important that herbalists learn about herbs and their medicinal uses. At this point, how they obtain the knowledge is left up to the herbalist's initiative.

Many of today's older and established herbalists learned their skills from grandparents, parents, and community herbalists. Originally the knowledge was passed down from generation to generation. Today, herbalists continue to learn the trade from experienced herbalists. The typical method for training is to complete an apprenticeship program with a master herbalist. Many accomplished herbalists will take on aspiring herbalists as apprentices and provide hands-on training. Herbalist students learn to identify, plant, grow, and harvest plants and herbs and make herbal teas, tinctures, oils, essences, capsules, salves, and other remedies from established herbalists.

Aspiring herbalists can find apprenticeships by networking with local herbalists or by contacting one of the several herbal professional associations. Locating apprenticeship training can be as informal as asking another herbalist to teach you all he or she knows. Apprenticeship training isn't necessarily an established program; it can be any training given by a working herbalist who is willing to share his or her knowledge. Though this may sound unstructured, it actually works quite well because often herbalists-in-training are getting one-on-one or small group education, and students get to choose an herbalist they are eager to work with.

Many herbalists offering apprenticeship programs also offer classes as part of the program. Typical topics covered during class training include: herbal therapeutics, botany, plant identification, herbal gardening, counseling skills, and business management. After completing an apprenticeship, students are usually awarded a certificate confirming their training as herbalist. Each herbal apprenticeship program or training school offers different certificates or diplomas. For example, a practical herbalism certificate is for people who want to become an herb retailer and grow, wildcraft, manufacture, and distribute herbs. A master or clinical herbalist certificate is for those who want to become an herbal practitioner and consult with people on health problems. Since each school and program is different, aspiring herbalists should research programs to find the one that meets their needs.

In addition to apprenticeship training, there are a variety of schools and correspondence courses that offer classes in herbal medicine. A few schools offer a typical classroom structure, but the majority of schools are correspondence schools. Correspondence schools are distance-learning programs where students complete self-study at home. Correspondence schools guide students in their studies and provide course outlines, texts, and requirements for completion. Most correspondence schools offer a hands-on component as part of the program. This varies from school to school, but it can mean spending a month on-site for practical training or going on weekends for six months. All of the schools differ in terms of cost, length of study, length and timing of practical training, and course requirements. Some students elect to go to herbal school abroad, where there are more training options.

Finally, some people study to become herbalists on their own. This approach is easiest for people who use herbs themselves, who garden as a hobby, and who, over time, focus their personal interest of herbs to studying their medicinal and scientific uses. People can learn a lot about the use and making of herbal remedies from the many books available on the subject. Reading alone is not enough, however. Some students elect to take a variety of workshops offered by herbalists to complement self-study. Although they may not be in a particular training program, students can piece together knowledge by attending professional development workshops designed for herbalists. They may take a few correspondence courses and seminars. One aspect that may be absent in this method of training is the study of the scientific and chemical constituents of plants. It is important for individuals to clarify their career goals before designing a self-study program.

Salary and Job Outlook

Salary varies greatly depending on the type of herbal business. An herbalist in private practice can charge anywhere from $30 to $100 an hour for individual consultation. The amount charged depends on geographic location and reputation of the herbalist. A typical fee would be approximately $50 an hour. Herbal clinicians don't usually spend all of their time in appointments, so the earnings would depend greatly on number of clients and outside activities the herbalist is involved in. Giving workshops and selling products are two ways to increase earnings. With herbal growers and retailers, the salary depends on the amount of herbs produced and number of clients. Economic success relies on the marketing effectiveness of each herbalist. Those who are effective at marketing and running their businesses do well financially and make a comfortable living.

The job outlook for the future is bright. As holistic health care increases in popularity, the demand for herbalists is growing. The outlook is fueled by consumer demand, and currently there is great consumer demand in certain parts of the country. Geography can play a role in the success of an herbal practice. In areas where holistic health care is thriving, herbalists do well. In some parts of the country there are no herbalists. Generally speaking, there are high concentrations of herbalists on the East and West Coasts and in the Southwest. Once a student is involved with the profession, it is easy to identify herbal-friendly states and communities.

Professional Organizations

American Botanical Council
www.herbalgram.org

American Herbal Pharmacopoeia
www.herbal-ahp.org

American Herbalists Guild
www.americanherbalistsguild.com

Herb Research Foundation
www.herbs.org

Schools

Check herbal and holistic health magazines for additional school listings; you can also contact the American Herbalists Guild (www .americanherbalistsguild.com).

American Association of Integrative Medicine
www.aaimedicine.com

American Institute of Aromatherapy and Herbal Studies
www.aromatherapyinst.com

Avena Botanicals
www.avenabotanicals.com

Blazing Star Herbal School
www.blazingstarherbalschool.org

California School of Herbal Studies
www.cshs.com

Connecticut Institute for Herbal Studies
www.ctherbschool.com

Dry Creek Herb Farm and Learning Center
www.drycreekherbfarm.com

East West School of Herbalism
www.planetherbs.com

North American Institute of Medical Herbalism
http://naimh.com

Northeast School of Botanical Medicine
www.7song.com

Rocky Mountain Herbal Institute
www.rmhiherbal.org

School of Natural Healing
www.schoolofnaturalhealing.com

7

Massage Therapy

Massage and other bodywork therapies promote physical, emotional, mental, and spiritual health through the use of human touch. Massage therapists use their hands and arms to manipulate and stimulate the body's muscles and tissues. Massage feels good and can alleviate or improve common health problems by stimulating lymph fluids, increasing blood flow, and eliminating toxins. It is a healthy, drug-free method for addressing various health problems, relieving stress, preventing disease, and maintaining health.

Philosophy

Massage therapy is an ancient and sacred healing method that began thousands of years ago. To touch someone in comfort or to rub an aching muscle is a natural instinct valued as a healing method throughout history and the world. Massage developed from the Eastern folk traditions of China and India. Peter Heinrik, a Swedish athlete and educator, brought massage to Western culture by developing Swedish massage, still the most popular form of massage. Today's massage has branched out into many forms, each with its own traditions. The philosophy that underlies and connects all massage is the belief in the healing power of human touch to comfort, care, relax, and improve the body's ability to heal.

Types of Clients and Problems

Most people come to massage for relaxation. They are stressed out with their jobs or problems at home. Other people have chronic pain, sore muscles from playing sports, are recovering from surgery, or are using massage as a supplement to physical therapy.
—Jennifer Jennings, Massage Therapist

Many healthy people go to a massage therapist simply because it feels good, but massage therapists also see people with a wide range of health issues. Massage is well known for reducing stress and relieving muscle aches. Other problems a massage therapist may work with include:

Anxiety	Intestinal problems
Tension headaches	Low back pain/spinal pain
Insomnia	Premenstrual syndrome
Muscle strains	Pain
Sciatica	Eye strain
Eating disorders	Abuse issues
Addictions	Body image issues
AIDS/HIV	Immune system disorders

In addition, massage offers many physical, emotional, and mental health benefits. Some of the physical benefits include:

- Increases circulation of blood and lymph fluids
- Increases joint flexibility and range of motion
- Relaxes nervous system and reduces the negative effects of stress
- Reduces blood pressure
- Nourishes skin
- Stimulates endorphins, the body's natural painkillers
- Improves body posture
- Strengthens immune system, which helps prevent disease
- Improves healing of sprained or pulled muscles and ligaments
- Reduces spasms, swelling, pain, and formation of scar tissue
- Promotes deeper and easier breathing
- Increases excretion of waste products, which improves digestion

Emotional and mental benefits include the following:

- Promotes deep relaxation and reduces mental stress
- Increases capacity for clear thinking
- Creates a relaxed state of awareness
- Creates a feeling of well-being
- Reduces anxiety
- Enhances self-image and self-esteem
- Satisfies need for caring touch
- Increases the mind/body connection
- Eases emotional expression

Massage therapists work with people of all ages, from newborns to the elderly. They work to meet the individual needs of a wide array of clients, although massage is not recommended for conditions such as certain circulatory problems, some types of cancer, cardiac problems, areas of hemorrhage, or recent fractures or sprains. Since massage therapists are not doctors and do not diagnose health problems, they act as a supplement to other forms of health care. Clients with more serious health problems use massage as an adjunct to other forms of treatment. For example, someone with high blood pressure could use massage in addition to other methods for controlling blood pressure. Clients with a serious illness such as AIDS may use massage as a way to reduce mental stress or to help the body deal with the physical stress of treatments. Some people use massage as a way to develop a positive attitude that undoubtedly affects health. Regardless of health status, most clients enjoy massage and find it helpful for their health goals.

It should be noted that although the word *therapist* is in the job title, massage therapists are not trained in psychology and do not provide talk therapy. Massage therapists who have additional schooling in psychology or counseling may combine their services, but as a rule massage therapists do not provide therapy. They are often caring and empathic people who will listen to their clients, but they are not trained to do psychotherapy.

Types of Massage

It's really an enriching experience. The effect massage has on people is really wonderful. And they keep coming back and coming back!

—Jennifer Jennings

Although massage therapists do not diagnose health problems, they do spend time in the beginning of each session asking clients about their health, medical history, previous or current medical treatments, stress levels, work, social life, and so forth. They want to find out why a client is seeking massage therapy and what he or she hopes to get out of it. This information helps the massage therapist decide what to focus on during the massage.

The average length of a massage is one hour, although sessions vary from half an hour to two hours in length. In some settings it can even be as short as fifteen minutes, such as chair massages offered in the workplace. The number of massage sessions depends on the therapist's method and the client's health goal. People who use it for relaxation may only get a massage when they are stressed. Others with certain health conditions need massages weekly or daily, as in the case with athletes. There is no typical length of treatment because massage is often used as a supplement to medical treatment. However, the therapeutic benefits of massage are cumulative—the more often a person gets a massage, a deeper level of relaxation is reached and the better he or she will feel.

The field of massage therapy has blossomed, and there are many therapeutic massage methods available today. Each massage method has its own techniques, theories, and philosophies. Some massage therapists focus on one method of massage, while others use a combination of techniques for working with clients. Typically, massage therapists are trained in one method of massage but may incorporate other techniques, depending on their training and client needs. Listed below are some of the popular therapeutic massage and bodywork methods.

Swedish Massage

This is the most common massage method in the United States used for general relaxation and muscle tension. A soothing full-body massage that uses long strokes and kneading techniques, it improves circulation and range of motion, removes muscle wastes, and increases flexibility. Swedish massage works from the belief that you always massage toward the heart for circulation benefits.

Neuromuscular/Trigger Point Therapy

This is a deeper form of corrective massage used to restore muscles to proper functioning. It uses concentrated finger pressure on specific areas to relieve pain or break spasms. It is also used for clients seeking deeper relaxation.

Deep Muscle Massage

Through slow strokes and deep finger pressure on specific areas, deep muscle massage releases tension in the body. Often used for treating muscle spasms, scar tissue, and chronic tension, it also can be used for specific problem areas or for a full-body massage.

Sports Massage

Sports massage therapists enhance an athlete's performance by increasing muscle flexibility and removing muscle waste. Using massage as a warm-up supplement can decrease the risk of injury. Sports massage is also used to reduce stress on the body that occurs from vigorous exercise and to assist in the healing of soft-tissue injuries.

Reflexology

Similar to acupuncture or acupressure, reflexology applies pressure to specific points on the hands and feet that are thought to correspond to different organs and areas of the body. Some massage therapists specialize in reflexology (called *reflexologists*), while others incorporate reflexology into a full-body massage.

Chair Massage

Chair massage is a type of massage that is showing up in work-places, shopping malls, health fairs, and trade shows. Therapists use their preferred massage techniques, but the massages are given in special chairs. Clients are fully clothed, and the typical on-site chair massage takes about fifteen minutes.

Rolfing

The goal of rolfing is to align the body along a vertical axis. The therapist (called a *rolfer*) uses thumbs, hands, and arms to realign, reeducate, and alter the length and tone of muscles. The therapy can be slightly painful, but this structural integration is believed to increase the health and effectiveness of body functioning.

Trager

The Trager method is a fluid, moving therapy that uses bouncing and light rocking movements to loosen joints, increase flexibility, and release physical and psychological tension.

Craniosacral Therapy

Craniosacral therapy is the massage of the bones in the face, neck, head, and skull. Bones and membranes are subtly manipulated to reduce tension and to treat headaches, ear infections, migraines, and jaw pain.

Shiatsu

This is a Japanese method of massage that uses deep pressure on meridian points along the body to increase the flow of chi or life energy. The therapist uses hands, elbows, arms, knees, and feet to apply rhythmic, deep pressure. Typically the client remains clothed.

Pregnancy and Infant Massage

Massage therapists specialize in pregnancy massage to help women with muscle pain, fluid retention, and other discomforts of pregnancy. Upon birth, infant massage therapists teach mothers massage techniques to increase newborn motor skills and bonding of mother and child.

Employment Settings and Working Conditions

A lot of massage therapists just starting out like to work in established practices so they don't have to worry about insurance, health codes, zoning laws, and getting an establishment licensed. Or they can go out on their own. Where I work, another person owns it and I pay a percentage of what I make. For me it is the perfect thing, working part-time and being a wife and mother.

—Jennifer Jennings

Massage therapists work in private practice or in group practices with other massage therapists and health practitioners such as doctors, nurses, physical therapists, psychologists, chiropractors, and acupuncturists. Massage therapists can be found in hospitals, nursing homes, health clubs, hotels, fitness centers, spas, beauty salons, and vacation resorts and on cruise ships. Some work as private therapists for the rich and famous. Increasingly, massage therapists are being hired by corporations to provide massage in the workplace in the attempt to reduce stress on the job and keep employees healthy. A few massage therapists teach at schools of massage.

Massage therapists have the flexibility to choose their own work settings and levels of responsibility. If they choose private practice, they have the added responsibility of running their own businesses. They are responsible for advertising and marketing their services, billing clients, keeping records, scheduling appointments, filing taxes, obtaining insurance coverage, and managing the office. Most massage therapists in private practice do everything themselves, where group practices may hire office employees, adding the responsibility of staff supervision, payroll, and employee benefits. Massage therapists in private practice can design their work environments and schedules and control the number of clients they see each week. Many massage therapists offer evening hours to be more accessible to working clients. Massage therapists in private practice work in offices that are relaxed, comfortable, and clean. Some work in their homes or go to clients' homes. Self-employed massage therapists typically earn more than do those who are not.

Besides self-employment, there are many other employment settings available. The conditions vary as working in a corporation is very different from working on a cruise ship. Corporations, health clubs, spas, cruise ships, and resorts often have massage therapists working on staff as salaried employees. Another avenue is contracting. Spas, health clubs, and corporations may contract a massage therapist on a part-time basis. In this case, therapists may work one day at spa, a few days at a health club, and one day at a corporation. In these situations massage therapists are still considered self-employed, but they have different responsibilities from those in private practice. A benefit of this profession is the various work scenarios available, and massage therapists can design their work life to meet their individual interests and needs.

As with work settings, the number of hours worked varies. Working full-time as a massage therapist doesn't mean doing eight hours of massage a day for five days a week. Massage is very hard work and can be physically and emotionally draining. It is difficult to stay mentally focused, and physically it is hard on muscles, hands, and back. Again, it is up to the individual therapist to determine how much work he or she can handle, but according to massage therapist Jennifer Jennings, three to five massages a day, five days a week is feasible.

The Profession

According to government statistics, there are about ninety-seven thousand massage therapists working as full- and part-time practitioners. Massage therapists practice in every state in the United States, and twenty-five states and the District of Columbia license them. Licensing and accreditation of schools have helped bring massage therapy into the public consciousness. Today, many people, including those who wouldn't normally consider alternative therapies, regularly schedule massages for themselves.

Training and Qualifications

You have to be caring and take into consideration that there are going to be overweight people, extremely thin people, and people with skin conditions and disease. You need to be able to see beyond the physicalness of it, which can be hard for some people to do. I can't imagine anything I'd rather be doing for a living.

—Jennifer Jennings

Most massage therapists enter the profession because they want to help people in a personal and meaningful way. Success as a massage therapist requires academic knowledge, technical and clinical skills, manual dexterity, sensitivity, interpersonal skills, communication skills, and a strong commitment to helping others. Knowledge of massage techniques combined with empathy and caring are important qualities for this career.

In 1992 a certification exam called the National Certification in Therapeutic Massage and Bodywork (NCTMB; www.ncbtmb .com) was created as the first nationwide method for credentialing massage therapists. This certification enhances a therapist's professional credentials. The approximately eighty thousand therapists holding this certification are required to participate in continuing education and professional development activity to stay current.

Although there are more than sixty accredited schools of massage in the United States, many others are not accredited by the American Massage Therapy Association (www.amtamassage.org). All programs accredited by the American Massage Therapy Association require at least five hundred hours of classroom instruction, with a minimum of three hundred hours of massage therapy techniques, one hundred hours of anatomy and physiology, and one hundred hours of additional required courses including first aid and CPR. Outside of these minimum requirements, programs vary in terms of philosophy, techniques, character, number of hours, and curriculum. States have requirements for practice, and schools often reflect these requirements.

Each school of massage has its own admission requirements, but typically applicants must have a minimum of a high school diploma or GED. Schools look for mature candidates who are physically, emotionally, and academically able to practice massage therapy and are in good health. Applicants must have a clear desire to help people and a motivation for massage therapy.

The length of time to complete massage therapy training can be from six months to one and a half years of full-time study. Many schools offer part-time evening or accelerated programs to make it available to working adults who are making a career change. The number of hours required for training varies between five hundred and one thousand hours.

Each school of massage will have its own unique curriculum, and candidates should carefully research schools, techniques, and philosophies to find schools that match their particular interests and goals. Sample courses in a massage training program include the following:

Reflexology	Communication skills
Neuromuscular therapy	Stress management
Sports massage	Meditation
Connective tissue massage	Legal and ethical issues
Mind/body connection	Practice management
CPR/first aid	

All programs include classroom instruction, lectures, demonstrations, paired practice, and clinical internships. Upon completion, therapists can continue their education to develop a specialty or to deepen their knowledge of the body and massage. Typical specialty areas include sports massage, infant massage, reflexology, shiatsu, structural bodywork, and mind/body massage.

Massage therapists are licensed in most states and practice in all of them. In states without state licensing, local or county governments regulate massage practice. Even in licensing states, local laws may still apply. Contact the city attorney, mayor, or county commissioner's office for information on regulations.

Salary and Job Outlook

Salaries can be influenced by the qualifications of the therapist, client satisfaction, number of years in practice (if self-employed), employment setting, and geographic location. In most cases, massage therapists receive payment from clients. Massage therapists charge between $35 and $130 per hour for a massage; some of this may go to the company/spa/facility for which the therapist works. The median income for massage therapists is between $25,000 and $40,000 a year, with some earning as much as $60,000 a year. Generally, massage therapists earn 15 to 20 percent of their income as gratuities; for those who work in a hospital or other clinical setting, however, tipping is not common. Some insurance companies will pay for massage if it has been prescribed by a physician.

Massage therapy is a growing field driven by consumer demand. According to the American Massage Therapy Association, consumers visit a massage therapist seventy-five million times each year. Legislative activity and increasing licensing laws also indicate the growth of this profession. With the increasing interest in preventive health by the public and an awareness of the negative effects of stress, massage therapy as a profession will continue to grow.

Professional Organizations

Acupressure Institute
www.acupressure.com

American Massage Therapy Association
www.amtamassage.org

Association of Bodywork and Massage Professionals
www.abmp.com

International Association of Infant Massage
www.iaim.net

International Institute of Reflexology
www.reflexology-usa.net

International Massage Association
www.imagroup.com

Rolf Institute
www.rolf.org

Trager Institute
www.trager.com

National Certification Exam Information

National Certification Board for Therapeutic Massage and
    Bodywork
www.ncbtmb.com

Massage Training Programs

The following schools are accredited or approved by the Commission on Massage Therapy Accreditation (COMTA; www.comta
.org). These programs have demonstrated compliance with the
COMTA standards by completing a rigorous process that included
a comprehensive self-study, on-site observation by external professionals and educators, and evaluation by an independent commission. Accreditation is for a limited time and, thus, must be
periodically re-earned. Programs may also be accredited by agencies in addition to COMTA.

Alaska

University of Alaska
www.uaa.alaska.edu

Arizona

Desert Institute of the Healing Arts
www.diha.com

California

Mueller College of Holistic Studies
www.mueller.edu

Colorado

Massage Therapy Institute of Colorado
www.mtic-co.com

Connecticut

Connecticut Center for Massage Therapy
www.ccmt.com

Delaware

The National Massage Therapy Institute
www.studymassage.com

District of Columbia

Potomac Massage Training Institute
www.pmti.org

Florida

Core Institute
www.coreinstitute.com

Educating Hands School of Massage
www.educatinghands.com

Florida College of Natural Health
www.fcnh.com

Florida School of Massage
www.floridaschoolofmassage.com

Sarasota School of Massage Therapy
www.sarasotamassageschool.com

Illinois

Chicago School of Massage Therapy
www.csmt.com

Kishwaukee College
www.kishwaukeecollege.edu

Morton College
www.morton.edu

National University of Health Sciences
www.nuhs.edu

Indiana

Alexandria School of Scientific Therapeutics
www.assti.com

Iowa

Carlson College of Massage Therapy
www.carlsoncollege.com

Kansas

BMSI Institute
www.bmsi.edu

Louisiana

Blue Cliff College
http://bluecliffcollege.com

Maine

Downeast School of Massage
www.downeastschoolofmassage.net

New Hampshire Institute for Therapeutic Arts
www.nhita.com

Maryland

Allegany College of Maryland
www.allegany.edu

Baltimore School of Massage
www.bsom.com

Massachusetts

Cortiva Institute
www.mtiweb.edu

Greenfield Community College
www.gcc.mass.edu

Springfield Technical Community College
www.stcc.edu

Michigan

Ann Arbor Institute for Massage Therapy
www.aaimt.edu

Lakewood School of Therapeutic Massage
www.lakewoodschool.com

Minnesota

Northwestern Health Sciences University
www.nwhealth.edu

Missouri

St. Charles School of Massage Therapy
www.spastcharles.com

Montana

Big Sky Somatic Institute
www.bigskysomatic.com

Health Works Institute
www.healthworksinstitute.com

New Hampshire

New Hampshire Institute for Therapeutic Arts
www.nhita.com

New Jersey

Academy of Massage Therapy
www.academyofmassage.com

Healing Hands Institute for Massage Therapy
www.healinghandsinstitute.com

Institute for Therapeutic Massage
www.massageprogram.com

The National Massage Therapy Institute
www.studymassage.com

Omega Institute
www.omegacareers.com

Somerset School of Massage Therapy
www.ssmt.org

New Mexico

Crystal Mountain School of Therapeutic Massage
www.crystalmtnmassage.com

North Carolina

Body Therapy Institute
www.massage.net

Oregon

East-West College of the Healing Arts
www.eastwestcollege.com

Pennsylvania

Baltimore School of Massage
www.bsmyork.com

Cortiva Institute
www.psmt.com

National Massage Therapy Institute
www.studymassage.com

Synergy Healing Arts Center and Massage School
www.synergymassage.com

Rhode Island

Community College of Rhode Island
www.ccri.edu

Tennessee

Institute of Therapeutic Massage and Movement
www.itmm.info

Roane State Community College
www.rscc.cc.tn.us

Virginia

Cayce/Reilly School of Massotherapy
www.edgarcayce.org

National Massage Therapy Institute
www.studymassage.com

Virginia School of Massage
www.vasom.com

Washington

Brenneke School of Massage
www.brennekeschool.com

Brian Utting School of Massage
www.busm.edu

West Virginia

Mountain State School of Massage
www.mtnstmassage.com

Wisconsin

Blue Sky School of Professional Massage
www.blueskymassage.com

Lakeside School of Massage Therapy
www.lakeside.edu

8

MIDWIFERY

MIDWIVES ARE TRAINED maternity care professionals who provide prenatal care, attendance at childbirth, postpartum care, education, counseling, and support for women and families during the pregnancy and childbearing process. They care for women who are likely to have uncomplicated pregnancies and deliveries. Historically, midwifery has always existed. The word *midwife* means "with woman" in Old English. Years ago, before hospitals and medical technology, all women had midwives for giving birth. In many countries, midwifery is the only birth option, with midwives delivering 80 percent of the babies born worldwide. In the United States, the percentage is much lower, approximately 5 percent, but more and more women are considering midwifery as a childbirth option.

Childbirth is one of the most powerful experiences for a woman and her family. Many women are interested in making the process individual, creative, and unique to themselves and their family. Midwifery encourages and allows women to design their own birth process while keeping the safety of the child and mother the first priority. For women considering midwifery, there are two options: lay or independent midwives, and certified nurse midwives.

Lay or independent midwives are midwives who primarily work in home settings with women and families who want a home birth. They are trained in all aspects of maternity care, but they are not physicians or nurses and are typically not associated with a hospital. They focus on a natural birth process and minimize outside interventions such as drugs, epidurals, episiotomies, and other invasive procedures that are unnecessary during normal births.

Certified nurse midwives are traditionally trained nurses who receive additional training in midwifery. The certified nurse midwife was developed in the United States and Canada. In other parts of the world, nursing training is not required to be a midwife. Certified nurse midwives tend to work in hospitals, birth centers, and clinics, and a small number work in homes. They also are concerned with a healthy, natural birth process, but due to their medical training, they can be more likely to use medical intervention. The certified nurse midwife appeals to many women because of the security of a hospital birth in conjunction with the benefits of midwifery. Most midwives are women.

Philosophy

The body knows exactly what to do. The way the baby grows and develops, and how labor progresses—a woman's body was designed for childbirth. A midwife has to trust, respect, and believe in the power of the body.

—Cilia Bannenberg, Midwife

Midwifery is based on the fact that pregnancy and childbirth are normal, healthy, natural events. Childbirth is not considered a medical condition or a health problem, and thus within safety limits, midwives are committed to a philosophy of nonintervention during childbirth. They believe in a natural birth process free of medical and technological intervention, medication, and unnecessary medical procedures. They believe in the body's functioning and trust the woman's body to do what it is supposed to do during birth. They are committed to safe health care and childbirth. In the event of complications or high-risk pregnancies, lay midwives refer clients to physicians and hospitals and continue to support the woman during birth. This accounts for only about 10 percent of midwifery births with approximately 90 percent of births being normal and problem free.

Midwives believe in a woman's right to take responsibility for her delivery. The pregnant woman is trusted and viewed as the one in charge of her birth. The midwife is a coach, counselor, teacher, and advocate rather than an "expert" who is going to control the birth. Midwives view family members as part of the experience, and family participation and support is encouraged throughout the entire pregnancy and birth process. Midwives also expect women to be responsible during pregnancy with regard to lifestyle choices and in planning the birth process.

Types of Clients

All types of women go to midwives for their prenatal care and delivery, although one characteristic that is common among women who seek midwives is a sense of personal responsibility. Women who go to midwives don't expect the midwife to do the delivery for them or to make it easier for them with medication. They tend to be women who are prepared to maintain a healthy lifestyle to maximize their ability to have a natural childbirth. They often have clear ideas about how they want to give birth and are very active in the entire process. Women who want to have a home birth have no other option than to go to a midwife.

Lay midwives have restrictions on the types of clients they will work with. Because their goal is to facilitate a natural childbirth, they typically don't take on clients at high risk for complications. This includes women with kidney disease, diabetes, drug addiction, heart disease, hypertension, severe anemia, severe infection, toxemia, placenta previa, Rh sensitization, twins or multiple births, or other health problems that cause abnormal presentation during pregnancy. Midwives also restrict having a home birth to between thirty-seven and forty-two weeks of pregnancy. Anything before thirty-seven weeks is too premature to have at home because the baby's lungs are not fully developed. After forty-two weeks also poses risk for complications. Some midwives refuse to work with women who smoke, drink, or don't watch their diet and nutrition during pregnancy. Any woman who is assessed to be at risk for birth complications is referred to an obstetrician and hospital birth.

Types of Care Rendered

During labor I bring out my birthing stool and I ask the woman if she wants to try it. I tell the woman to do whatever she needs to do to be comfortable. We try to have fun in between the contractions. During labor I monitor mom and the baby, and when the baby is born, I do a newborn exam.

—Cilia Bannenberg

Midwives care for a pregnant woman throughout her whole pregnancy, during birth, and after birth. The biggest difference between a lay midwife and a certified nurse midwife or obstetrician is time. Lay midwives spend a great deal of time with clients. It begins with prenatal care. Prenatal care is considered vital for the pregnant woman. The midwife spends at least one hour a month with her clients until the seventh month of pregnancy. The hour-long visits are markedly different than the ten and fifteen minutes obstetricians and some certified nurse midwives have to spend with clients. Visits become bimonthly during the seventh and eighth month and weekly thereafter until the onset of labor. During this time the midwife monitors the health of the mother and baby and provides education and counseling. Midwives are trained to do the same things as certified nurse midwives or obstetricians. They do pelvic exams, Pap smears, health status exams, fetal heart-rate monitoring, and blood work. In addition they spend a great deal of time on education. They educate mothers about nutrition, exercise, fetal development, and the birth process. They typically provide or arrange for prenatal birthing classes, breastfeeding classes, and newborn classes and are constantly educating the woman and her family about the changes happening to her body. The midwife provides a great deal of counseling and emotional support during this time.

Labor and birth is the second major area of care given by midwives. Lay midwives deliver babies in home settings or in freestanding birth centers. Both the mother and the baby are carefully monitored and cared for throughout labor and birth. The type of birth depends on individual client needs and desires, and midwives work with women and their families to create the birth that they want, within safety limits. Midwives offer home births, water births, or delivery at birthing centers. They use different tools than hospitals for making the birth as comfortable as possible. Some midwives use birthing stools, which women can sit on to have their babies. Other women want to lie in bed, be in the bathtub, walk, play music, dance, eat, or do a variety of other things during labor. The midwife supports women during labor and tries to make it as fun and relaxing as possible.

During the birth process, the midwife guides the woman and baby through the birth. In a normal birth, the pregnant woman does the work and the midwife acts as a support. She will help the woman through the birth and catch the baby. All along, the midwife, who is trained to handle emergency situations, is watching for complications. Emergencies during a home birth are rare, but in the case of serious complications, the midwife will make arrangements and accompany the woman to the hospital. The midwife will also remain there with the mother-to-be as a support. In most cases, however, once the baby is born, the midwife cuts the umbilical cord, delivers the afterbirth, and completes a newborn exam. Then the family celebrates!

After birth, midwives refer newborns to a pediatrician within a few days. They also provide postpartum care to the woman and her family. This includes counseling and education on well-baby care, breastfeeding, dealing with siblings, parenting, and any other issue the family may have. They typically plan for the completion of the birth certificate and report the birth to the appropriate health departments. They also conduct a four- to six-week postpartum exam, which includes a pelvic exam and Pap smear for the mother and another check for the baby and family.

Midwives and clients often develop intimate relationships because of the time spent with each other. Midwives strive to get to know the family so everyone will feel comfortable when it comes time for the birth.

Employment Settings and Working Conditions

*As a midwife, you are always on call, and that means you have
a hard time planning for other things. I can't just pick up and go
away for a couple days, and it is hard getting up at 2:00 A.M.
Although it is very demanding, it's also extremely rewarding. I
just love it!*

—Cilia Bannenberg

In the United States, lay midwives do not work in hospitals. They
are primarily self-employed working out of private offices or their
homes. Some work in independent birthing centers and others form
group practices working with other midwives, childbirth educators,
breastfeeding counselors, doulas (birthing assistants), nutritionists,
and counselors. Midwives can also be found teaching at midwifery
schools or teaching childbearing classes and related workshops. A
few write or get involved with other income-providing aspects of
midwifery, such as selling midwifery-related tools like birthing
stools, water-birth tubs, and educational material.

Midwives typically keep clean, warm, and comfortable offices
because they want to provide a pleasing environment for their
clients, as well as themselves. Their work schedules vary greatly
depending on the number of clients they have and when women go
into labor. Midwives have control over their schedules with regard
to prenatal care and scheduling appointments, which gives them a
lot of flexibility in organizing their day. What they don't have control over is when they deliver babies. Midwives are constantly on
call, twenty-four hours a day, every day, so the work can be unpre-
dictable and untimely. Midwives must organize their lives to be

available on a moment's notice, and this is something aspiring midwives must consider before entering the profession. Midwives typically wear beepers so they can be reached at all times, and they often work with clients within a restricted geographic region to ensure that they can get to clients quickly.

In addition to caring for clients and families, midwives run their own businesses. They are responsible for marketing and advertising their services. Marketing is necessary to maintain clientele, although many clients come from word of mouth and repeat business. Midwives also handle billing, record keeping, and taxes.

One of the challenges for lay midwives is the struggle for acceptance by the medical establishment and society. Most women in the United States are socialized to have their babies in a hospital under the care of a doctor. This ingrained system creates the need for lay midwives to defend their legitimacy. The satisfaction of their clients and a belief in the philosophy of natural childbirth compensate for the difficulty of being seen as an alternative approach to childbirth.

Training and Qualifications

I took a difficult route where I had to be very disciplined. I enrolled in a year-long course in Massachusetts, where I went to class one day every three weeks and did a lot of home study. I took anatomy and physiology at the University of New Hampshire, and I did my practical training in Holland. I had to do my training this way because I have a family and couldn't just pick up and move to study at a midwifery school.

—Cilia Bannenberg

There are several paths to becoming a lay midwife. Typically training takes the form of textbook study, classes, and an apprenticeship with an experienced midwife. One avenue, called *direct entry*, is to attend a midwifery school offering a traditional educational environment. The Seattle Midwifery School (www.seattlemidwifery .org), for example, offers a three-year training program. This includes classes on basic health/nursing skills, embryology and fetal development, genetics, gynecology and women's health, midwifery care, midwifery counseling skills, perinatal nutrition, pharmacological and alternative treatments, assessment of women, and a clinical seminar. After completion of courses in a classroom setting, students undertake an internship with an experienced midwife. Being a nurse or having health care training is not required to be a lay midwife, although midwifery programs may have other prerequisites for admission. These can include courses in anatomy and physiology, biology, nutrition, or some relevant women's health care experience. A traditionally designed midwifery school offers a structured path for becoming a lay midwife.

Other options for midwifery training require independent learning. Many programs are designed to offer a flexible, albeit independent approach to learning. These programs typically include a number of correspondence courses in which the student conducts independent study and research. In addition to independent study, daylong, weeklong, or occasional weekend workshops are offered to supplement the home study. Finally, an apprenticeship is required, which is usually set up by students in their home areas. This approach to training works well for nontraditional students who need a more flexible training program, or for those who do not live in close proximity to a midwifery school. The challenge of these programs is the self-discipline required to maintain studies and learn independently.

Another option for aspiring midwives is to piece their training together rather than attend one specific program. The midwifery profession is governed at the state level, each having its own laws and requirements to practice midwifery. All aspiring midwives should contact their state governments to learn about these requirements. Upon doing this, some students follow their state requirements as a guideline for their training. With this approach, aspiring midwives can use multiple avenues for training as long as they complete all the requirements. For example, a student might take a class at a local college, take a few courses at one or several midwifery schools, and then organize an apprenticeship with a local midwife. Again, this allows a great deal of flexibility and control over training but requires a lot of research and legwork to put together an individual training program.

As mentioned above, individual state law regulates lay midwifery. State laws and training requirements should be researched before beginning midwifery training. Upon completion of training, most states require passing an exam to receive a practice license or certificate. On a national level, Midwives Alliance of North America (MANA; www.mana.org), the largest midwifery professional association, has an exam and is working toward national certification. MANA also accredits midwifery schools, and attendance and completion of training at a MANA-accredited school earns graduates the title of Certified Professional Midwife. This title is not required to be a midwife, but it can make the process of meeting state requirements easier, as well as being a credential to demonstrate competency to clients.

There are also many programs available for registered nurses who want to become certified nurse midwives. The main requirement for certified nurse midwives is being a registered nurse. Typically one must work as a nurse before returning to school to specialize in midwifery. In some cases registered nurses attend one of the MANA-accredited midwifery schools and return to working in the hospital setting. Usually nurses attend programs that are specifically designed to award the credential of certified nurse midwife. These schools are often associated with hospitals. There are nine- to twelve-month certificate programs and programs awarding a master's degree in nurse midwifery. The master's degree usually takes sixteen to twenty-four months. The American College of Nurse Midwives (ACNM; www.midwifery.org) both oversees and approves certified nurse midwife programs.

Salary and Job Outlook

People are certainly becoming more aware of midwifery. You see it with the popularity of supplements and herbs people are taking. They are more aware of different health care options, midwifery, and home births.

—Cilia Bannenberg

A number of variables can affect salaries for midwives, including the type of practice setting (private practice, hospital, birth center, home birth, health clinic), geographic part of the country, type of location (urban or rural), benefits packages offered with salary, hours worked per week, and type of care provided (full scope of women's health services, prenatal care, gynecologic care, and so forth). The salary of a lay midwife also varies depending on the number of clients she can attract. Most women do not enter this profession for the financial rewards, and midwives tend to have reasonable fees that are much lower than the cost of a traditional hospital birth. A typical fee for a midwife is approximately $2,000 per birth. Midwives tend to charge one fee, which encompasses the entire package of care: prenatal, birth, and postpartum care. The yearly salary depends on the number of women in the area having babies and how well the midwife can market her services. Many midwives in private practice start their business slowly. Twelve to fifteen births a year could be considered the equivalent of working part-time. There are midwives working in clinics or group practices who deliver many babies each month. The earning potential varies depending on geographic location, proximity to hospitals, work setting, and competition from other midwives or certified nurse midwives.

Insurance coverage of midwifery services will help increase the number of women who can afford to use a lay midwife. Currently, most clients pay out of pocket. Some insurance companies are starting to cover lay midwifery services because it is more cost effective compared to hospital births.

Certified nurse midwives often earn higher salaries than lay midwives because they tend to work for hospitals or obstetric groups. A typical salary for a nurse midwife is $55,000 to $80,000 annually. They also receive benefits and can have a more structured schedule because they share being on call with other doctors and certified nurse midwives. Insurance companies typically cover certified nurse midwife care.

Currently health care is the largest-growing area of the employment sector. It is difficult to tease out exactly how fast the midwifery area is expanding. With the overall growth in health care and the increasing interest in holistic alternatives, it appears midwifery will continue to grow. More and more women are turning to midwifery because they view midwives as more personal than busy obstetricians. The drug-free and noninstitutional settings are an appealing alternative for many women. In addition, the sustained popularity of midwifery in other countries demonstrates the timelessness of this profession.

Professional Organizations

Many states have their own midwives associations (some are listed below). Contact your local state departments of Health and Human Services for more information.

American College of Nurse Midwives
www.midwife.org

Midwifery Education Accreditation Council
www.meacschools.org

Midwives' Alliance of North America
www.mana.org

Doulas of North America
www.dona.org
(An association for labor support providers)

International Childbirth Education Association
www.icea.org

La Leche League International
www.lalecheleague.org
(A breastfeeding information and support organization)

Massachusetts Friends of Midwives
www.mfom.org

Massachusetts Midwives Alliance
www.massmidwives.org

New Hampshire Midwives Association
www.nhmidwives.org

MANA-Accredited Midwifery Schools

Bastyr University
www.bastyr.edu

Birthingway College of Midwifery
www.birthingway.edu

Birthwise Midwifery School
www.birthwisemidwifery.org

Florida School of Traditional Midwifery
www.midwiferyschool.org

Maternidad La Luz
www.maternidadlaluz.com

Miami Dade College
www.mdc.edu

Midwives College of Utah
www.midwifery.edu

National College of Midwifery
www.midwiferycollege.org

National Midwifery Institute
www.nationalmidwiferyinstitute.com

Seattle Midwifery School
www.seattlemidwifery.org

ACNM-Accredited Nurse Midwifery Programs

Baystate Medical Center
www.baystatehealth.com/midwiferyed

California State University (Fullerton)
http://nursing.fullerton.edu

Case Western Reserve University
http://fpb.cwru.edu

Columbia University
http://cpmcnet.columbia.edu/dept/nursing

East Carolina University
www.nursing.ecu.edu

Emory University
www.nurse.emory.edu

Frontier School of Midwifery and Family Nursing
www.midwives.org

Georgetown University
http://snhs.georgetown.edu

Marquette University
www.wi-cnm.net

Medical University of South Carolina
www.musc.edu/nursing

New York University
www.nyu.edu/nursing

Ohio State University
www.con.ohio-state.edu

Oregon Health and Science University
www.ohsu.edu/son/nmw

Philadelphia University
www.instituteofmidwifery.org

San Diego State University
http://nursing.sdsu.edu

Shenandoah University
www.su.edu/nursing

University of California–San Francisco
http://nurseweb.ucsf.edu

University of Cincinnati
http://nursing.uc.edu

University of Colorado
www.uchsc.edu

University of Florida
http://con.ufl.edu

University of Illinois at Chicago
www.uic.edu/nursing

University of Indianapolis
http://nursing.uindy.edu

University of Kansas
www2.kumc.edu/midwife

University of Maryland
http://nursing.umaryland.edu

University of Medicine and Dentistry of New Jersey
www.umdnj.edu

University of Miami
www.miami.edu

University of Michigan
www.nursing.umich.edu

University of Minnesota
www.nursing.umn.edu

University of New Mexico
http://hsc.unm.edu

University of Pennsylvania
www.nursing.upenn.edu

University of Rhode Island
www.uri.edu

University of Washington
www.son.washington.edu

Vanderbilt University
www.mc.vanderbilt.edu/nursing

Wayne State University
www.nursing.wayne.edu

Yale University
http://nursing.yale.edu

9

HOLISTIC MEDICINE

HOLISTIC DOCTORS ARE traditionally trained medical doctors who have incorporated holistic philosophies and alternative healing methods into their practices. Holistic medical physicians are similar to traditionally practicing physicians in that they have attended the same four years of medical school, completed two to six years in a residency program, and are licensed to practice medicine in all fifty states. They have all the privileges and status that come with being a medical doctor. Holistic doctors and traditional doctors work in the same hospitals, treat the same diseases, are part of the American Medical Association (www.ama.org), and practice all aspects of medicine. What differentiates holistic doctors from traditional doctors is their philosophy regarding health. They look at the body as a whole and work to enhance its natural healing abilities. Also, holistic doctors have received additional training in alternative health care methods and offer different options in treating patients.

Philosophy

Holistic medicine did not develop as a field from one specific theory or historical tradition; it is currently a developing specialty area for physicians. With the rise of holistic medical alternatives available in the United States and the popularity of these methods with consumers, traditionally trained physicians began to take notice. Many traditional doctors have become interested in alternative health care options and have sought additional training in holistic philosophies, theories, and methods. More recently, some people who want to practice holistic health care choose to get an M.D. degree for the credibility, although they plan to practice holistic medicine.

Like all holistic health care providers, holistic doctors view health in a different way from traditional doctors. Holistic doctors believe that there is more to health than the elimination of diseases or symptoms. They look at the whole person and work to find underlying causes of illness. They educate and encourage patients to take responsibility for their health. Although some holistic doctors use pharmaceuticals and traditional treatments, they also have faith in the body's natural healing abilities. The goal of the holistic doctor is to use the least-invasive methods to support the body's ability to heal itself.

Each holistic doctor has his or her own unique philosophy of health care. Some use traditional medicine in combination with holistic alternatives, while others dedicate their practice to holistic medicine. Since physicians come to holistic medicine from various backgrounds and differ in the amount of alternative methods they use, there isn't one blanket philosophy for this unique, individual, and constantly changing group of professionals.

Types of Patients and Problems

Holistic doctors treat patients with all types of health problems, from simple colds to more serious conditions. Any health care provider can work in a holistic way, so the types of problems and patients seen depends on the specialty area of the physician. For example, a gynecologist, a cancer specialist, a family practitioner, a heart surgeon, an internist, and a pediatrician can all work holistically. Holistic doctors still see patients in their specialty areas, but they use a holistic frame of reference for diagnosing and treating patients. Other holistic practitioners may leave their specialty area and set up a practice to focus on holistic care. In these cases, holistic doctors tend to see patients with chronic conditions that historically have not been helped by traditional medical approaches. Chronic conditions include arthritis, allergies, back pain, immune system disorders, degenerative diseases, and chronic pain. Chronic diseases are the strength of holistic doctors, although any patient can benefit because of the goal to improve both the immune system and overall health.

Types of Treatment

I consider myself to have an integrated practice where I utilize homeopathy, acupuncture, bodywork and manipulation, hypnosis, herbal medicine, progressive relaxation, and a lot of attitude work.

—Dayton Haigney, M.D.

The amount and type of holistic care provided varies among doctors. As licensed physicians they have the flexibility to create their own practice using traditional and alternative treatment methods. Holistic doctors may use treatments such as homeopathy, nutrition counseling, acupuncture, acupressure, herbology, massage and bodywork, counseling, ayurveda, hypnosis, therapeutic touch, yoga, vitamin/mineral supplements, meditation, and energy healing.

Some holistic physicians use traditional diagnosing and treatment methods such as x-rays, blood tests, lab work, drug treatments, and surgery. In addition they may offer holistic methods as a supplement to traditional treatment. For example, a heart surgeon may use traditional medical methods and perform heart surgery, but he or she may add yoga, massage, and hypnosis to the patient's treatment plan. Many holistic physicians see the value of both approaches to medicine and are using a combination of services to help patients. These doctors are starting to bridge the gap between the medical and holistic health community and tend to be in high demand by consumers who want both.

The second group of holistic doctors view holistic care as their primary service and rely on holistic diagnosing and treatment methods. These physicians spend a great deal of time with patients. An initial appointment typically takes one to one and a half hours, and follow-up appointments last at least half an hour. In this case, a holistic doctor may diagnose problems by taking a detailed health history and asking patients about symptoms, diet, sleep patterns, stress levels, work and personal life, allergies, and use of alcohol, drugs, tobacco, and caffeine. They would then use diagnosing methods specific to their holistic training and specialty. If physicians were trained in acupuncture, they would use Chinese medical diagnosing and treatment methods. If they studied herbs, they could incorporate herbalism into a treatment plan. The type of treatment depends on the holistic training of the physician and the individual patient's needs. Finally, with training and expertise in traditional and alternative medicine, holistic doctors refer patients to a wide range of practitioners, if necessary.

Holistic doctors are in a unique position in health care. With a turf battle going on between the medical and holistic communities, a holistic doctor has a foot in each camp. This appeals to many patients who want the security of seeing an doctor but want to try holistic alternatives. These physicians will influence the future of medicine by helping holistic health care gain credibility while educating traditional physicians on the value of offering a wide range of health care services.

Employment Settings and Working Conditions

In my own practice, most of my patients have primary care physicians, so I don't take emergency calls. I work Monday through Friday nine to five in this one-room office. People can call me at home, and I don't feel this is intrusive. The lifestyle is wonderful, although I could make more money on the allopathic [traditional] side.

—Dayton Haigney

Holistic doctors work in many different settings. They work in hospitals, clinics, private practices, and group practices. Some do research, write, and teach at medical schools or holistic training schools. As licensed physicians, holistic doctors have the flexibility to work in any arena.

Physicians who use holistic methods as their primary means of care tend to work in private practice. They may work individually or in group practices with other holistic health care practitioners such as nutritionists, massage therapists, or herbalists. Holistic doctors in private practice, like all self-employed professionals, have the responsibility of running a business. They handle advertising and marketing, bill patients and insurance companies, keep records, and supervise staff. Many in private practice have office employees working for them and are responsible for office management.

Holistic doctors in private practice have the freedom to design their own work styles. They work in offices that are professional and comfortable and can make their own schedules. Many work the traditional workweek, but some choose to work four days a week or offer evening hours. Holistic physicians working in hospitals or clinics may have less control over their time and have on-call hours.

The stress level in this field is significant. It can be very stressful for holistic physicians to work in a profession that is not typically supportive of holistic medicine or alternative ways of healing. Since they are trained and often work with traditional doctors, holistic physicians are a minority in the field and are surrounded by colleagues who may not understand or support holistic methods. Holistic doctors must be comfortable knowing that they are working outside of mainstream medicine. They often have to look for support of their work elsewhere. In addition, being involved in the major health decisions of people's lives can be a lot of pressure.

Training and Qualifications

It can really become tough for a student because you won't get support for holistic medicine in medical school. You have to be committed, centered, and strong enough to know that you're out of the mainstream.

—Dayton Haigney

Currently there is no direct route for becoming a holistic medical doctor. There are no medical schools specializing in holistic medicine. To obtain the M.D. degree, candidates must follow the traditional route for attending medical school. Students must meet prerequisite requirements and take the MCAT to be eligible for admission to medical school. Medical school takes four years to complete. Upon completion of medical school, students must undertake residency programs, which last one to six years. Typically a minimum of two years is required for licensure. Since there currently is no holistic residency program available, students complete residency programs in all different aspects of medicine.

The essential ingredient for becoming a holistic doctor is knowledge. Obtaining knowledge and training in holistic medicine is up to the initiative of the aspiring holistic practitioner. To become a holistic doctor, the traditionally trained physician needs to take the initiative to learn holistic philosophies and methods completely on his or her own.

There are many different avenues for training. The level of holistic training depends on the physician's interest, time, and money to devote to further education. The route to becoming a holistic doctor is different for each person, but there are many options available to work toward this goal. Some suggestions include:

1. When choosing a medical school, choose one that appears more open to mind/body beliefs. There are medical schools that offer at least one course on holistic or alternative medicine. (See list of schools at end of chapter.)

2. Since there are no holistic residencies, students should choose residencies based on their interests. Many physicians who are interested in holistic health care choose residencies in family medicine. If possible, choose residencies in hospitals and universities that are more open to new ideas. A few hospitals have holistic medical departments, and the National Institutes of Health (www.nih.gov)

recently opened an office for holistic medicine. In time, more hospitals may begin to offer holistic health care departments.

3. The crucial element is to receive training in holistic methods. Either before, during, or after medical school, take classes in holistic medical approaches. Training options include taking classes at naturopathic medical schools, schools of acupuncture/Oriental medicine, schools of chiropractic, schools of osteopathic medicine, or other schools offering training in the holistic area of interest. In addition, physicians can receive training by attending professional development conferences, workshops, and seminars on holistic medicine. An excellent way to obtain training is to work as an apprentice under a holistic practitioner. Getting practical training in addition to course work is necessary to practice holistic medicine.

4. Join the American Holistic Medical Association (www.holis ticmedicine.org) and other holistic professional associations to learn about training opportunities, make contacts with other holistic professionals, and stay current on what is going on in the field.

Because there are no regulations regarding holistic medical training for a licensed physician, it is the responsibility of the physician to select the holistic areas of interest and to seek out training. The length of time for training varies from physician to physician. Some physicians do intensive training once they have completed traditional medical school and licensing requirements; others start a practice and slowly pick up training in holistic approaches over time. There is no right way to reach the goal of becoming a holistic doctor. Each person will have his or her own unique path, and if truly committed to the philosophy of holistic health, he or she will find the right training.

Salary and Job Outlook

The employment outlook for holistic medical doctors is excellent. One reason is the growing popularity and demand by the public for alternative approaches to health care. This demand is fueling the growth of all holistic medical fields. Holistic medical doctors are especially in demand because the M.D. degree provides a legitimacy that many consumers seek. People who have been using traditional medicine their entire lives tend to be more comfortable seeing a holistic practitioner who is also an M.D. In addition, holistic doctors are in demand because they are covered by insurance companies. Many consumers seeking holistic medical care prefer to find practitioners whom their insurance companies will cover, and holistic doctors are covered more readily than other holistic practitioners. Holistic doctors are in the unique position of having both traditional and holistic training, and they are often seen as "the best of both worlds," which increases their demand.

Holistic physicians, like traditional doctors, can earn a good salary. The salary depends on the style of practice, hours worked, and number of patients seen. A typical range would be $90,000 to $140,000. Some holistic physicians earn additional income from selling nutritional supplements, herbs, or other holistic products.

Professional Organizations

American Academy of Medical Acupuncture
www.medicalacupuncture.org

American Holistic Health Association
www.ahha.org

American Holistic Medical Association
www.holisticmedicine.org

National Center for Complementary and Alternative Medicine
http://nccam.nih.gov

Medical Schools Offering Courses in Alternative Therapies

Boston University School of Medicine
www.bumc.bu.edu

Case Western Reserve University School of Medicine
www.meds.cwru.edu

Columbia University College of Physicians and Surgeons
www.cumc.columbia.edu

Emory University School of Medicine
www.med.emory.edu

George Washington University School of Medicine
www.gwumc.edu

Georgetown University School of Medicine
http://som.georgetown.edu

Harvard Medical School
www.hms.harvard.edu

Indiana University School of Medicine
www.medicine.iu.edu

Johns Hopkins School of Medicine
www.hopkinsmedicine.org

Medical College of Pennsylvania
www.philadex.com

Michigan State University
www.msu.edu

Mount Sinai School of Medicine
www.mssm.edu

Pennsylvania State University College of Medicine
www.hmc.psu.edu/college

Rush Medical College
www.rush.edu

Southern Illinois University School of Medicine
www.siumed.edu

Stanford University School of Medicine
www.med.stanford.edu

Temple University
www.temple.edu

Tufts University School of Medicine
www.tufts.edu/med

University of Arizona School of Medicine
www.medicine.arizona.edu

University of California, San Francisco School of Medicine
http://medschool.ucsf.edu

University of Cincinnati School of Medicine
www.med.uc.edu

University of Louisville School of Medicine
www.louisville.edu/medschool

University of Maryland School of Medicine
http://medschool.umaryland.edu

University of Miami School of Medicine
www.miami.edu

University of Rochester School of Medicine
www.urmc.rochester.edu

University of Virginia School of Medicine
www.med.virginia.edu

Wayne State School of Medicine
www.med.wayne.edu

Yale School of Medicine
www.yale.edu

10

NATUROPATHIC MEDICINE

NATUROPATHIC MEDICINE IS a system of primary care that combines traditional and holistic methods to achieve optimal heath and wellness. Naturopathic physicians (N.D.s) are trained in all of the same sciences as medical doctors, but they also study holistic approaches to health care with an emphasis on disease prevention. Naturopathic physicians use therapies that are almost exclusively natural such as homeopathy, nutrition, acupuncture, botanical medicine, and counseling. Naturopathic medicine is based on the fact that the human body has an innate power to heal itself, and naturopathic physicians use treatments to support the body's inherent self-healing abilities.

Philosophy

We look at the body as an intelligent whole and symptoms as the way the body communicates. For example, when your nose is running, your body is communicating an infection. Finding and treating the cause of the symptom is what naturopathic medicine is all about.

—Leon Hecht III, Doctor of Naturopath

Naturopathic medicine dates back to the eighteenth and nineteenth centuries and is one of the oldest forms of medicine, existing long before today's technological and pharmaceutical advances. It was brought to the United States in the late 1800s by Benedict Lust, a German doctor who founded the first naturopathic medical school in New York. Naturopathy developed quickly and was booming in the 1920s, with more than twenty schools of naturopathic medicine in the country. The field began to decline in the 1940s and 1950s with the growth of allopathic medicine and the pharmaceutical industry. In recent years, renewed interest in holistic health and dissatisfaction with conventional medicine have staged a comeback for naturopathy.

Naturopathic physicians combine natural approaches from a variety of health care traditions. The foundation of naturopathic medicine is embedded in six philosophical principles of healing. Although they use an eclectic range of healing methods, naturopathic physicians are unified by the following philosophies:

1. **The healing power of nature.** Naturopathic physicians recognize the body's inherent ability to fight disease and restore and maintain health. They work to support this process by identifying and removing obstacles to bolster the patient's healing capacities.

2. Treat the whole person. Naturopathic physicians recognize the harmonious functioning of all aspects of an individual as essential to health. They consider the complex interaction of physical, mental, emotional, genetic, spiritual, environ- mental, and social factors in diagnosing and treating illness.

3. First, do no harm. Naturopathic physicians respect the body's ability to heal and consequently use the least-invasive, least-toxic treatments possible. They are aware of the side effects of treatments and try to use gentle and nondisruptive methods. Naturopathic physicians avoid treatments to solely suppress symptoms, as it may interfere with the healing process.

4. Identify and treat the cause. Naturopathic physicians seek to treat the causes of disease rather than to eliminate specific symptoms. Symptoms are seen as signs that the body is out of balance and is trying to heal itself. When only the symptom is treated, the underlying causes remain and can manifest in other more serious health problems.

5. Prevention is the best cure. The primary objective of a naturopathic physician is the attainment of optimal health and the prevention of disease. Naturopathic physicians work with patients to assess risk factors, heredity, and susceptibility to disease and make recommendations to prevent illness.

6. Doctor as teacher. The original meaning of the word *doctor* is "teacher." The objective of the naturopathic physician is to educate patients and help them take responsibility for their own health by making good choices.

Types of Patients and Problems

Naturopathic physicians are trained as general practitioners and primary care physicians. Thus, they treat patients with a broad range of health problems, from the common cold to acute and chronic conditions. Naturopathic physicians are often viewed as the M.D.s of holistic medicine and provide care to patients with all types of health problems.

In addition to providing comprehensive care, there are many areas naturopathic physicians can specialize in. Some specialize in treating patients with chronic degenerative diseases such as diabetes, hypertension, and arthritis. Other areas include nutritionally based problems, women's health issues, candida, neurological and structural problems, chronic fatigue syndrome, immune system disorders, allergies, gynecological problems, and muscular problems. Their greatest strength lies in preventive medicine, acute illnesses, natural childbirth, clinical nutrition, and chronic illnesses that have not responded well to other medical approaches. Research studies support the benefit of naturopathic medicine for patients with AIDS/HIV, heart disease, arthritis, and cancer. Although naturopaths are trained in bone setting and x-ray, they typically do not treat broken bones. They refer patients who need major surgery, acute trauma care, cast settings, or prescription medication to allopathic doctors. In general, naturopaths are not allowed to prescribe drugs, although in some states they have prescription rights for certain classes of drugs.

Naturopathic physicians treat patients of all ages from newborns to the elderly. Some people choose naturopathic medicine after traditional medicine has failed. Other people see naturopathic physicians as a first choice to prevent disease and maintain health or as an alternative to traditional medicine. Naturopathic physicians receive a large number of their patients through patient referrals, and it is not uncommon for a naturopathic physician to see entire families.

Types of Treatment

Like medical doctors, naturopathic physicians are trained, licensed, and skilled to use traditional methods for diagnosing problems through blood/urine lab testing, x-rays, and physical exams. They also use alternative methods for diagnosing patient problems. The first appointment with a naturopathic physician can take up to one and a half hours because an extensive individual and family health history is taken in addition to the physical exam. In fact, patients are often asked to fill out questionnaires prior to their appointments. Naturopathic physicians ask their patients about their presenting problem; symptoms; any past treatments; use of vitamin supplements; allergies; medical history; diet and eating patterns; sleep patterns; use of alcohol, drugs, caffeine, and tobacco; stress levels; exercise levels; type of lifestyle; occupation; and social life. Naturopathic physicians attempt to assess a patient's physical, mental, emotional, and spiritual state in order to provide the most effective care.

Naturopathic medicine is not so much a separate form of health care, but a combination of many forms of alternative therapy. Once a diagnosis is made, naturopathic physicians choose between a wide array of treatments based on the individual needs of the patient and the specialty area of the physician. One or more treatment methods can be used. Treatment options include:

- **Clinical nutrition.** "Food is the best medicine" is the basis of naturopathic medicine. Naturopathic physicians use nutritional counseling and recommend dietary changes and nutritional supplements to treat—or be part of the treatment—of many medical problems.

- **Physical medicine.** Naturopathic physicians utilize the manipulation of muscles, bones, and spine to treat illness. They may use massage, ultrasound, exercise, gentle electrical pulses, and hydrotherapy (the use of hot and cold water).
- **Homeopathic medicine.** Naturopathic physicians use homeopathic treatments to strengthen the body's immune system to promote a lasting cure for health problems. Homeopathic therapies are medicines made from highly diluted natural substances, where the substance that produces symptoms in healthy adults cures those same symptoms in ill adults. The remedies work on the body's energy level to strengthen the life-force energy.
- **Botanical medicine.** Naturopathic physicians use plant substances and herbal remedies to treat patients. Botanical medicine can address a number of problems simultaneously, and since they are organic substances, they are compatible with the body's chemistry and can be effective with very few toxic side effects.
- **Naturopathic obstetrics.** Naturopathic physicians who specialize in obstetrics provide natural childbirth in nonhospital settings. They provide education and counseling in addition to prenatal, delivery, and postnatal care. They minimize outside interventions during childbirth and work to strengthen the woman's body to prevent pregnancy complications and to deliver healthy babies.
- **Chinese medicine.** Many naturopathic physicians use acupressure and acupuncture to treat patients by restoring balance to the energy system. The mind/body philosophy of traditional Chinese medicine is similar to the naturopathic physician's philosophy of healing.
- **Psychological medicine.** Naturopathic physicians attend to the psychological aspects of their patients because they believe mental attitude and emotional state can influence and perhaps even

cause physical illness. Naturopathic physicians provide counseling, nutritional balancing, stress management, hypnotherapy, biofeedback, and various other therapies to help patients heal on the psychological level.

• **Minor surgery.** As general practitioners, naturopathic physicians do in-office minor surgery. They use local anesthesia, repair superficial wounds, and remove foreign bodies, cysts, and other superficial masses.

• **Environmental medicine.** Some naturopaths specialize in detoxification of the body to help patients eliminate toxic or chemical substances that result from environmental exposure.

Because of the training in traditional and holistic medicine, naturopathic physicians interact with a diverse number of health care professionals, including traditional medical doctors. They are not opposed to drugs, major surgery, or traditional medicine when these methods are necessary. They make and receive referrals to other practitioners in the best interest of the patient.

Employment Settings and Working Conditions

When you choose to be a naturopathic doctor, you need to be aware that you are also going to run a business and you need business savvy. I entered this profession very naive about that— I was going to heal the world, which is the most gratifying part— but running the business can be almost as much work as the rest of it.

—Kristy Fassler, Doctor of Naturopath

Most naturopathic physicians are in private practice. Some teach and conduct research at schools of naturopathic medicine. A few are involved in doing research and advise the National Institutes of Health (www.nih.gov). Others work for natural product companies as consultants or sales representatives. As naturopathic medicine gains ground in the political arena and as acceptance by traditional medicine and society increases, naturopathic physicians may be found in hospitals, clinics, and other traditional health care arenas.

Naturopathic physicians primarily work individually or in group practices. Group practices may also include other health care practitioners such as nutritionists, massage therapists, herbalists, or acupuncturists. Naturopathic physicians working in private practice or in small practices have the responsibility for running the business as well as treating patients. They are responsible for advertising and marketing, billing patients and insurance companies, keeping records, and supervising staff. Naturopathic physicians usually have office employees working for them and are responsible for all aspects of employee management.

The work setting is professional, clean, and comfortable. Naturopathic physicians work a schedule similar to other primary care physicians, seeing patients during a typical workday. Because of the demand for naturopathic medical services and the low number of naturopathic physicians who are practicing, naturopathic physicians have a tight schedule, with new patients often waiting months for an appointment.

Naturopathic physicians tend to locate in areas where holistic medicine is recognized and accepted and in states where they can be licensed. There are areas of the country where there are no naturopathic physicians. Naturopathic physicians should research geographic areas carefully in deciding where to practice, as the level of acceptance varies.

The Profession

There are approximately two thousand licensable naturopathic physicians in the United States. The American Association of Naturopathic Physicians (AANP; www.naturopathic.org) represents approximately five hundred licensed naturopathic physicians. With three professional schools of naturopathic medicine in the United States, the field is graduating several hundred more every year. Naturopathic physicians are licensed in eleven states, although they practice in many other states under different regulations. The profession is well organized and the AANP is the leading organization to support and further the field of naturopathic medicine.

Training and Qualifications

One of the biggest challenges in choosing to be a naturopathic doctor is financial. Education is very costly and you graduate with a lot of debt. Then you need a loan to start a practice, and it takes a while to break even.

—Kristy Fassler

Currently there are only a few schools of naturopathic medicine in the United States and Canada. Admission is competitive and typically a bachelor's degree is required. Students must have prerequisite courses in premedical chemistry and physics, organic chemistry, biology, psychology, social science, humanities, English, and writing. Schools look for mature candidates with strong moral character and a commitment to naturopathic medicine. The degree awarded is the N.D.—Doctor of Naturopath. Training takes four to five years. In the first two years, students take courses in anatomy and physiology, psychology, philosophy of naturopathic medicine, clinical diagnosis, homeopathy, pharmacology, nutrition, orthopedics, and immunology. In the third and fourth year, students study obstetrics, Chinese medicine, medical genetics, cardiology, minor surgery, botanical medicine, pediatrics, therapeutic exercises, emergency medicine, ear/nose/throat, gastroenterology, geriatrics, neurology, urology, oncology, dermatology, medical ethics, and they take business practice seminars. The training also includes a series of clinical internships. In addition to the four years of training, some naturopathic medical students elect to take a fifth year in a specialty area such as obstetrics or homeopathy.

Prospective students should be aware of some confusion regarding naturopathic education. The AANP accredits and recognizes schools of naturopathic education in the United States; these are the only training programs that lead to licensure. There are a variety of other programs that award an N.D. degree that do not meet accreditation guidelines. These programs are often correspondence schools with no clinical training or uniform curriculum standards. Students considering programs other than those recognized by the AANP should conduct thorough research to be sure the program meets their needs and goals. These alternative N.D. programs can provide useful training in health and wellness education, but they do not train individuals to be physicians. Only physicians with degrees from the three recognized naturopathic medical schools are eligible for licensure.

Naturopathic physicians practice under various legal provisions in almost every state with varying guidelines. The states that currently have licensing laws for naturopathic physicians are:

Alaska
Arizona
California
Connecticut
District of Columbia
Hawaii
Idaho
Kansas
Maine
Montana
New Hampshire
Oregon
Utah
Vermont
Washington

Many states are realizing the benefits of having physicians trained in preventive medicine and are considering legislation. The AANP is working to expand the licensing and availability of naturopathic physicians. Its goal is to have licensing in all fifty states.

Naturopathic physicians must pass a standard examination called NPLEX (Naturopathic Physicians Licensing Examination), which is required by all licensing states. The test includes five basic science exams covering anatomy, physiology, pathology, biochemistry, microbiology, and immunology, and these are taken after the first two years of study. Clinical exams are taken after the fourth year of study. They include clinical and physical diagnosis, lab diagnosis and diagnostic imaging, nutrition, physical medicine, pharmacology, botanical medicine, homeopathy, psychology, lifestyle counseling, minor surgery, and emergency medicine. Depending on the state, additional exams may be given in jurisprudence and acupuncture.

Because this is such a small field, naturopathic physicians are actively involved in the professional growth of their career area. Naturopathic physicians work with states and their professional organizations to encourage others to join the profession and secure licensing for naturopathic physicians.

Salary and Job Outlook

This profession is going to just boom! The demand is already there, and there are way too few of us to serve the demand.

—Kristy Fassler

Naturopathic medicine is a growing field with excellent prospects for new professionals. There is an increasing demand from the public for naturopathic medical services and a small number of physicians to meet the demand. During the first four years of practice, naturopathic physicians earn approximately $50,000 to $60,000 and after six to ten years $80,000 to $100,000. Naturopathic physicians collect their salaries directly from patients and insurance companies. Patients primarily pay for service, but more and more insurance companies are covering naturopathic medicine. Some states have passed laws requiring insurance companies to cover naturopathic medical services. This is expected to continue as insurance companies realize it is cost effective to use natural treatment methods and prevent disease.

Professional Organizations

American Association of Naturopathic Physicians
www.naturopathic.org
(AANP represents licensable naturopathic physicians in the United States. It supports legislation to license and regulate naturopathic physicians in all states and provides a referral service.)

American Naturopathic Medical Association
www.anma.com

Association of Accredited Naturopathic Medical Colleges
www.aanmc.org

Licensing Information

Federation of Naturopathic Physicians Licensing Authorities
www.fnpla.org

Naturopathic Physicians Licensing Examination Board
www.naturopathic.org/licensure/nplex.aspx

North American Board of Naturopathic Examiners
www.nabne.org

Naturopathic Medical Schools

Bastyr University of Natural Health Sciences
www.bastyr.edu

Boucher Institute of Naturopathic Medicine
www.binm.org

Canadian College of Naturopathic Medicine
www.ccnm.edu

Natural College of Naturopathic Medicine
www.ncnm.edu

Southwest College of Naturopathic Medicine and Health Sciences
www.scnm.edu

University of Bridgeport College of Naturopathic Medicine
www.bridgeport.edu/naturopathy

11

OSTEOPATHIC MEDICINE

OSTEOPATHIC MEDICINE IS a complete system of health care. Osteopathic physicians, like allopathic physicians (M.D.s) attend four years of medical school, complete two to six additional years in a residency program, and are licensed to practice medicine in all fifty states. Doctors of osteopathy (D.O.s) and allopathic physicians work in the same hospitals, treat the same diseases, belong to the American Medical Association, and practice all aspects of medicine. What differentiates an osteopathic physician from an allopathic physician is philosophy, emphasis on preventive medicine, and specialized training in the musculoskeletal system and manipulative techniques.

Philosophy

Osteopathy is a system of medicine founded by Dr. Andrew Taylor Still, M.D., in 1874. Dr. Still was dissatisfied with medicine at that time, which was based primarily on surgery and medication. He believed that there was more to health than administering medication and that the body had its own store of chemicals to heal itself. He emphasized the relationship between the musculoskeletal system and the organ systems and viewed the vascular (blood) and nervous systems as the key mechanisms responsible for health. The blood and nervous systems are how the body communicates and regulates its organs. The osteopathic philosophy holds that disease disturbances in the spinal column are carried through blood and nerves to different parts of the body where the problem will manifest. This relationship between structure (spine and nervous system) and function (organ/tissue functions) became the basis of osteopathic medicine.

Osteopathic physicians believe in a holistic philosophy where the patient is seen as a whole person in which mind, body, and spirit work together to influence health. Rather than just treating specific symptoms or illnesses, osteopathic physicians view the patient as an integrated, interrelated whole. They understand how the body's systems work together and pay special attention to the spine and nervous system, which influences the health of all other body systems. This focus gave rise to the osteopathic techniques of structural manipulation. The theory holds that hands-on manipulation of the musculoskeletal system will affect functioning in other areas of the body. Osteopathic physicians use manipulation techniques to increase blood circulation and nerve supply to organs, and this assists in restoring health. They trust the body's natural healing ability and use manipulation, medication, education, counseling, and other techniques to stimulate the body to heal. They believe the body has an innate tendency toward health and will naturally work to return to homeostasis after an illness or trauma. The first goal of the osteopathic physician is to prevent disease by educating patients; the second goal is to facilitate a return to health by stimulating the body's healing abilities.

Types of Patients and Problems

Like allopathic doctors, osteopathic physicians treat patients with all types of health problems, from simple colds to more serious conditions. Osteopathic medical schools focus on preparing physicians for family practice because of their belief in preventive medicine. They believe that if family practitioners work with patients to prevent disease, specialists wouldn't be as needed. Thus over half of osteopathic physicians work as primary care or family practitioners. However, osteopathic physicians can specialize in more than seventy broad specialty areas such as pediatrics, internal medicine, sports medicine, surgery, psychiatry, obstetrics, geriatrics, rural medicine, ear/nose/throat, cardiology, and ophthalmology. Osteopathic physicians treat patients of all ages, ranging from newborn to the elderly, and it is common for an osteopath to treat an entire family.

Types of Treatment

> *Osteopathy teaches us to use all of our senses. One of the major senses we have is touch, so we can diagnose and treat with our hands. The idea of using hands is a powerful tool, and it facilitates change in a patient at all levels: the spirit, the mind, and the matter.*
>
> —Tim Kingsbury, Doctor of Osteopathy

Like allopathic physicians, osteopathic physicians use traditional methods such as blood and lab tests, x-rays, and physical exams to diagnose problems. They also use extensive questioning for diagnosing patient problems. Osteopathic physicians spend up to one hour with new patients. During this time, an individual and health history is taken. Osteopathic physicians ask patients about the presenting problem; symptoms; past treatments; use of vitamin supplements; allergies; use of alcohol, drugs, caffeine, and tobacco; level of exercise; stress level; lifestyle; and social life. They seek to understand their patients on the physical, emotional, and mental levels to make accurate diagnosis and treatment plans.

In treating patients, osteopathic physicians use many of the same methods as allopathic physicians. As complete physicians, osteopathic physicians are trained and licensed to prescribe medication and perform surgery. They also have the freedom to utilize acupuncture, homeopathy, herbal medicine, and other holistic methods because they are licensed physicians. Unique to osteopathic physicians is their use of osteopathic manipulative treatment (OMT), a hands-on technique to diagnose and treat health problems. OMT requires osteopathic physicians to use their hands to manipulate nerves, muscles, and bones to facilitate proper bodily functioning and health. This involves gentle movement of joints, application of pressure on body organs and tissues, body positioning, muscle massage, rapid adjustments, and cranial manipulation. Research has found osteopathic manipulation to be particularly useful with musculoskeletal problems, chronic pain, arthritis, spinal and joint disorders, sports injuries, rheumatism, fibromyalgia, stress, respiratory infections, headaches, pneumonia, bronchitis, and nerve problems.

It should be noted that not all osteopathic physicians utilize manipulative treatments. Some osteopathic physicians consider manipulation as central to their practice and actively follow the philosophy outlined by Dr. Still. These physicians do not align themselves with traditional doctors and believe osteopathy has something uniquely different to offer patients. The other osteopathic physicians align themselves with mainstream medical practitioners and use osteopathic approaches only as a secondary component to allopathic treatments. These physicians appear more like allopathic doctors and may or may not use manipulation techniques. Osteopathic education is one route for becoming a licensed doctor. Some choose this route to become licensed but don't emphasize the philosophy or methods in their practice.

Finally, osteopathic physicians educate patients. They teach patients about developing healthy attitudes and lifestyles to prevent illness. This discussion includes nutrition education, stress management, and counseling. Osteopathic physicians spend a lot of time with their patients and are known for providing compassionate and preventive care.

Osteopathic physicians have a strong network of health care providers in their referral system. Being similar to allopathic doctors in their work and training, they refer to a wide range of traditional medical practitioners and services. With their holistic philosophy, they also make referrals to holistic and mental health practitioners.

Employment Settings and Working Conditions

The body heals itself by maintaining balance. I try to maintain a balance in my life. Unlike other osteopathic physicians, I decided to have a fairly limited practice in that I work four days per week, I don't carry a beeper, I don't work in hospitals, I make house calls, and I try to work with patients on a more personal level.

—Tim Kingsbury

Osteopathic physicians work in all the same places as allopathic doctors. They fit into all health care settings and work in hospitals, clinics, private practice, and group practices. Historically, osteopathy has been known for providing primary care in rural and underserved areas. In addition to medical practice, some osteopaths research, write, and teach at medical schools. Since osteopathic medicine is accepted by mainstream medicine and society, osteopathic physicians don't face the same challenges as other holistic health care providers. They have the flexibility to work in any health care arena.

Being trained first as primary care physicians, many osteopathic physicians work in private family practices either individually or with other osteopathic or allopathic physicians. Group practices may also include nutritionists or mental health counselors. Osteopathic physicians in private practice, like any self-employed professional, have responsibilities other than treating patients. They also run a business. They handle advertising and marketing of services, bill patients and insurance companies, keep records, and supervise staff. Most osteopathic physicians have employees working for them and are responsible for office management.

Osteopathic physicians have flexibility to design their work life if they go into individual private practice, but most work typical doctors' office hours plus on-call emergency shifts. Osteopathic physicians working in hospitals and clinics have a more varied schedule, which can require evening and weekend shifts, on-call shifts, and less control over their time. As licensed physicians, osteopaths have many options for finding or creating the work setting they desire.

There is a significant amount of responsibility and stress in this profession because osteopathic physicians are involved in major decisions in people's lives from birth to death.

The Profession

There are approximately thirty-eight thousand osteopathic physicians practicing in the United States, compared to six hundred thousand allopathic physicians. Like its more traditional allopathic counterpart, osteopathy is expected to grow faster than the average for all occupations through 2014. More than 50 percent of all osteopathic physicians are in family practice, internal medicine, pediatrics, and obstetrics/gynecology. Many serve areas of need working in small towns and rural areas. Osteopathic physicians are found in every state, with Florida, Michigan, Missouri, New Jersey, Ohio, and Texas having the highest concentrations. Osteopathic physicians are licensed to practice in all fifty states.

Training and Qualifications

Medical school training is the most challenging and stressful thing you are ever going to do in your life. But that's nothing compared to getting out there and doing the work. I like the challenge, autonomy, and constant learning. Each day when I come to work, my patients are my teachers.

—Tim Kingsbury

Currently there are twenty schools of osteopathic medicine in the United States accredited by the Bureau of Professional Education of the American Osteopathic Association, which is recognized by the U.S. Department of Education and the Council on Postsecondary Education. To meet the requirements for admission, students typically have a bachelor's degree with prerequisite courses in biology, physics, chemistry, organic chemistry, English, and psychology. Students from all majors are eligible to apply if the prerequisite requirements are met. The Medical College Admission Test (MCAT) is also required.

Schools look for individuals who are dedicated, mature, compassionate, and empathic and who have a strong desire to help people as an osteopathic physician. Many applicants have volunteer or work experience in a health care field. Prospective candidates are interviewed to determine if they are the right match for the school and profession. Superior grades at the undergraduate level and high scores on the MCAT are necessary due to the high level of academic study required.

Osteopathic medical school takes four years to complete and awards the Doctor of Osteopathy (D.O.). During the first two years, students take courses in basic clinical sciences such as:

Geriatrics	Anatomy and physiology
Microbiology	Pharmacology
Biochemistry	Community medicine
Pathology	Nutrition
Pediatrics	Osteopathic manipulative medicine

The third and fourth years focus on hands-on clinical training and research. Students participate in clinical rotations at affiliated hospitals, health centers, clinics, and offices of osteopathic physicians. Under the supervision of osteopathic physicians, students learn to provide patient care in family practice, pediatrics, surgery, internal medicine, rural medicine, obstetrics and gynecology, psychiatry, and other primary care fields.

Upon completion of medical school, students (now D.O.s) serve a one-year internship to enhance their clinical skills in internal medicine, family practice, pediatrics, surgery, and obstetrics/gynecology. The goal of training in these areas is to ensure that osteopathic physicians are trained to handle multiple health needs and practice as primary care physicians. Osteopathic physicians can then choose to take a residency program, which takes two to six years to complete, in a specialty area such as pediatrics, surgery, radiology, pathology, or internal medicine. Osteopathic physicians seeking board certification in a specialty may spend up to seven years in residency training, depending on the specialty. A final examination immediately after residency or after one or two years of practice also is necessary for certification by a board member of the American Board of Medical Specialists (ABMS) or the American Osteopathic Association (AOA). The ABMS represents twenty-four specialty boards, ranging from allergy and immunology to urology. The AOA has approved eighteen specialty boards, ranging from anesthesiology to surgery. For certification in a subspecialty, physicians usually need another one to two years of residency.

To become licensed and eligible to practice, all osteopathic physicians must pass state medical board examinations. Each state sets its own requirements, but typically the four years of training plus three years of clinical work are required.

A physician's training is costly. According to the Association of American Medical Colleges (www.aamc.org), in 2004 more than 80 percent of medical school graduates were in debt for educational expenses.

Salary and Job Outlook

Like allopathic physicians, osteopathic physicians earn a profitable salary ranging from $70,000 to $100,000 for family practitioners. Osteopathic physicians working in specialty areas can earn much more. Osteopathic physicians are covered by insurance companies and receive third-party payments. With the growth of health maintenance organizations (HMOs), primary care osteopathic physicians have more career options and higher salaries as HMOs shift away from specialists and require patients to go through primary care physicians. This trend is helpful for osteopathic physicians who tend to work in the primary care role.

Osteopathic medicine is a growing field with excellent prospects for new professionals. As licensed physicians they have enormous opportunities for medical practice, and licensure provides the freedom to design a practice and influence salaries.

Professional Organizations

American Academy of Osteopathy
www.academyofosteopathy.org

American Association of Colleges of Osteopathic Medicine
www.aacom.org

American College of Osteopathic Family Physicians
www.acofp.org

American College of Osteopathic Internists
www.acoi.org

American College of Osteopathic Obstetricians and Gynecologists
www.acoog.org

American College of Osteopathic Surgeons
www.facos.org

American Osteopathic Academy of Sports Medicine
www.aoasm.org

American Osteopathic Association
www.osteopathic.org

American Osteopathic Healthcare Association
www.aoha.org

Osteopathic Medical Colleges

Arizona

A. T. Still University College of Osteopathic Medicine
www.atsu.edu

Midwestern University
www.midwestern.edu/azcom

California

Touro University College of Osteopathic Medicine
www.tucom.edu

Western University of Health Sciences
www.westernu.edu

Florida

Lake Erie College of Osteopathic Medicine
www.lecom.edu

Nova Southeastern University
http://medicine.nova.edu

Georgia

Philadelphia College of Osteopathic Medicine
www.pcom.edu

Illinois

Midwestern University
www.midwestern.edu/ccom

Iowa

Des Moines University
www.dmu.edu

Kentucky

Pikeville College
http://pcsom.pc.edu

Maine

University of New England
www.une.edu/com

Michigan

Michigan State University
www.com.msu.edu

Missouri

Kansas City University of Medicine and Bioscience
www.kcumb.edu

Nevada

Touro University College of Osteopathic Medicine
www.tucom.edu

New Jersey

University of Medicine and Dentistry of New Jersey
http://som.umdnj.edu

New York

New York College of Osteopathic Medicine
http://iris.nyit.edu/nycom

Ohio

Ohio University College of Osteopathic Medicine
www.oucom.ohiou.edu

Oklahoma

Oklahoma State University Center for Health Sciences
http://osu.com.okstate.edu

Pennsylvania

Lake Erie College of Osteopathic Medicine
www.lecom.edu

Philadelphia College of Osteopathic Medicine
www.pcom.edu

Tennessee

Lincoln Memorial University DeBusk College of Osteopathic
   Medicine
www.lmunet.edu

Texas

University of North Texas Health Sciences Center at Fort Worth
www.hsc.unt.edu

Virginia

Edward Via Virginia College of Osteopathic Medicine
www.vcom.vt.edu

West Virginia

West Virginia School of Osteopathic Medicine
www.wvsom.edu

12

YOGA

YOGA IS AN ancient science of physical, mental, and breathing exercises used to promote health, well-being, and personal growth. It involves stretching, strengthening, and relaxing poses or postures (called *asanas*). Yoga stretches and tones muscles, joints, the spine, and the skeletal system as well as internal organs, glands, and the nervous system. In addition, yoga uses mental and breathing exercises to reduce stress and create unity of the body, mind, and spirit. Yoga breathing clears the mind and creates a state of relaxation. Yoga literally means "joining" or "union"—union of the body, mind, spirit, and universe. It encourages both inwardness and self-understanding and can bring about spiritual connections. Yoga is not a religion, but it can deepen any individual spiritual practice.

Philosophy

Yoga is the practice of removing tension in the body through movement, stretching, and breathing exercises. It is a way of surrendering to the breath and being able to sit with a quiet mind.
—Marj MacLaughlin, Yoga Instructor,
Massage/Energy Therapist

Yoga is known to be at least three thousand years old. It originated in India as one of the six Indian arts to achieve personal enlightenment. One of the most famous ancient books on the subject, *Bhagavad Gita*, was written around 200 B.C. Over time, yoga has developed into different schools and disciplines, each with its own theories and philosophies. All forms of yoga share the connection of the body, mind, and spirit. Some believe yoga brings a connection to God or other spiritual powers. It is holistic because it works to balance and strengthen the whole person. Yoga instructors teach people techniques to improve health and overall wellness and to prevent illness from occurring.

Types of Clients and Problems

Usually people come to yoga because of something physical, but there are often energy and mental blocks behind the physical problem. It all works together to free up the mind and body.
—Marj MacLaughlin

Yoga instructors work with people with a wide range of needs and goals. Some people come to yoga for the physical benefits—to remain flexible and fit. Others try yoga to help alleviate or improve certain health problems such as tension headaches or backaches. Many want to learn yoga to manage stress and increase relaxation. Yet others seek yoga for the mental benefits of a peaceful mind and sense of well-being. People with anxiety or other emotional problems use yoga to quiet the mind, look inward, and increase self-understanding, confidence, and the ability to cope. Some people come to yoga because they have a sense they aren't getting enough out of life. Yoga helps people feel whole and connect with all aspects of themselves. It also helps people pray or connect with spiritual beliefs.

Yoga is an individual experience and attracts a wide range of people each with his or her own reasons, hopes, and goals for doing yoga. While this may seem like a tall order for a yoga teacher, instructors don't specifically address these problems or goals. Through teaching of yoga, the benefits come. Yoga instructors don't have to be experts in these areas, and they don't counsel clients. They believe in the benefits of yoga and teach clients the techniques so each person can reach his or her own goals. Part of yoga is the client creating a goal for himself or herself, whether it's to feel fit, to relax, to relieve health or emotional problems, or to just have fun.

In recent years, medical research has begun to show the health benefits of yoga. Regular practice of yoga can help relieve such diverse conditions as:

Fatigue/low energy	High blood pressure
Arthritis	Chronic fatigue syndrome
Asthma	Back and neck pain
Addiction	Fibromyalgia
Insomnia	Heart conditions
High cholesterol	High blood sugar

Respiratory problems	Arteriosclerosis
Hypertension	Premenstrual syndrome
Pain	Infertility
Menopause	Weight management
Stress	Emotional/mental issues
Headaches	Stomachaches
Circulatory problems	Anxiety

Yoga is effective in increasing the body and mind's ability to cope with stress and the resulting health problems or health problems that lead to stress. It improves the body's natural healing abilities as well as directly relieving many symptoms. Practiced regularly, yoga is an effective method of preventive medicine.

Yoga instructors teach people of all ages and health status. Instructors offer specialized classes for groups of people such as children, the elderly, pregnant women, and people with heart conditions. They usually teach group classes for beginner, intermediate, and advanced clients and some offer individual one-on-one instruction. While yoga benefits everyone, more women than men take yoga classes.

Aspects of Yoga

Yoga instructors teach the yoga poses—the postures or asanas—which stretch and strengthen the body. Many people think of headstands or back bends when they think of yoga postures. These are examples of yoga postures, but yoga includes a wide variety of postures and movements that are both relaxing and challenging. There are postures done lying down, sitting, standing, and moving. Each posture has its own benefit to the body. Yoga teachers include a variety of postures in each class to meet the diverse needs of clients.

Breathing techniques, or *pranayama*, are another important tool yoga instructors use when working with clients. Breathing exercises relax tense muscles, flush the body with oxygen, and release the mind from stress. Breathing regulates the life-force energy in the body and helps clients gain energy for certain postures. There are different breathing exercises to meet specific needs. There are exercises for relaxation, energy, meditation, and for working through physical knots, anxiety, and mental stress. Some breathing techniques are done while lying down or sitting quietly, while others are used in conjunction with postures.

Finally, meditation is an important aspect of yoga instruction. Yoga instructors incorporate meditation at the end of a yoga class to complete total body/mind relaxation. Some yoga teachers specialize in meditation and lead meditation classes. Simply put, meditation is learning how to quiet the mind and let go of daily thoughts, worries, and stress. Meditation seeks a sense of peacefully living in the moment, and it can stimulate creative, intuitive, and problem-solving capabilities. It can increase self-acceptance, self-knowledge, and confidence by focusing inward, and it can increase spiritual connections. Meditation techniques involve using the breath, a vision or image, a sound, music, a *mantra* (repetition of a word), a prayer, or some other symbol. Every yoga teacher uses different methods to teach meditation to clients.

Yoga instructors facilitate the benefits of yoga by teaching the physical, mental, and breathing exercises to clients. There are many types of yoga, and each yoga teacher teaches different techniques based on his or her training and beliefs. No form of yoga is better than another. Each style offers a different path to meeting goals. Choosing the right yoga style is entirely a personal preference.

There are many other types of yoga. For example, *Kundalini* yoga uses the breath as its primary technique and is concerned with releasing the energy at the bottom of the spine. *Raja* yoga is yoga of the mind and primarily uses meditation techniques. The most popular form of yoga in the United States is *Hatha* yoga. Hatha yoga is yoga of the body and form. It focuses on physical postures, breathing techniques, and meditation to bring the body into a healthy state and relieve the mind and spirit from stress. Hatha yoga instructors teach exercise, breathing, and meditation techniques.

Employment Settings and Working Conditions

Finding space to teach is always hard in the beginning. You need to be flexible enough to throw your yoga mats in the car and run around to the YMCA or Knights of Columbus and teach wherever you can get a big space.

—Marj MacLaughlin

Most yoga instructors are self-employed and teach classes at various locations such as yoga centers, health clubs, hotels, resorts, schools, businesses, athletic facilities, mental health settings, hospice and senior care facilities, hospitals, addiction recovery programs, rehabilitation centers, and occupational and physical therapy centers. Some yoga instructors are paid as staff working full-time in these settings, while many others are running their own businesses offering classes as consultants. Most teach group classes; some offer private yoga lessons to clients. Some yoga instructors open their own yoga centers and offer a variety of services. Yoga instructors often team up with other holistic health practitioners to offer group services. For example a yoga center may also offer massage therapy, tai chi, energy healing, and nutritional services. Some instructors develop a specialty such as sports, prenatal, elder, or children's yoga. There is a great deal of flexibility for yoga instructors to design their work style and setting. Often new yoga teachers will start off teaching classes anywhere they can find work and space. They may then move to joining a group at a health center, opening their own yoga center, or becoming a staff member at a business, health organization, school, or other setting. Yoga is becoming increasingly popular, and it is not unusual to see yoga classes offered by corporations as a means of stress management. Finally, yoga instructors can become teachers for new yoga instructors and work at schools of yoga training.

As with any self-employed individual, self-employed yoga teachers are responsible for running their businesses, the largest part of which is marketing their services. Yoga teachers are also responsible for advertising and networking to develop a clientele. In addition, they are responsible for maintaining financial records of their expenditures and earnings.

The working conditions vary depending on the setting, but typically yoga teachers work in comfortable, quiet, open spaces. The schedule and hours depend greatly on the type of work life desired. Yoga teachers typically make their own schedules. Yoga teachers do not work the traditional forty hours a week teaching yoga. It would be nearly impossible to do yoga for eight hours a day, every day. Teachers working full-time teach approximately seven to ten classes a week. Classes are typically one to two hours long. The rest of their work time is spent on marketing their business and making contacts for consulting and outside activities. Many people teach yoga on the side as a second career. For example, it would not be unusual for a massage therapist to combine massage with teaching a few yoga classes per week. Yoga can also be a moonlighting job in addition to full-time employment.

Part of being a yoga teacher is having one's own yoga practice. Yoga teachers must believe and incorporate yoga into their daily lives. While an instructor may teach one class a day, part of the job is having a personal practice of yoga. This includes daily yoga at home and continual learning by taking yoga classes. There is always more to learn in yoga, and even the most advanced yoga teachers take classes to continually push themselves to reach higher levels of yoga skills and spiritual accomplishments.

The Profession

Working for yourself is a big benefit because you are able to create what you want every time you go to work. It is rewarding to help people take back the happiness in their lives instead of the stressed-out parts of themselves.

—Marj MacLaughlin

The yoga teaching profession is growing rapidly and becoming part of mainstream health and fitness fields. Many insurance companies, especially HMOs, cover the cost of yoga classes for clients, and yoga is found in traditional settings such as industry settings and health clubs. Although yoga is growing, there is little standardization of the profession. There are no national licensing or certification requirements. Thus there are no standardized requirements for becoming a yoga instructor. This may change in the future as yoga becomes a more standard health promotion practice.

Training and Qualifications

The best thing to do is to decide what kind of yoga you love and teach what makes you happy. There are a lot of different schools, and rather than just pick a school and get certified, I would suggest taking many classes with different people and developing your own yoga routine. Then find a school to match your style.

—Marj MacLaughlin

Prospective yoga teachers have many options for training because of the different types of yoga and yoga schools. Every program has its own philosophy, teaching methods, length and structure of training, and graduation requirements. Typically, training programs award degrees, diplomas, or certificates of completion.

The first step to choosing a yoga-training program is to decide on a yoga style. Taking yoga classes with many different instructors is a good way to explore the different types of yoga. It is helpful for aspiring yoga teachers to have knowledge about the different types of yoga to make an informed decision for training. The next step is to research yoga training programs. Current yoga teachers can usually recommend programs, and many other schools are listed in *Yoga Journal* (www.yogajournal.com). The best method for finding a program is to ask a yoga teacher whose style you find appealing where he or she studied and what other schools offer similar training.

Yoga teacher training programs vary in terms of length, cost, topics covered, and yoga styles. Most offer flexible schedules such as weekend training courses or two-week-long sessions with additional independent study. Others can be as long as two years. The Yoga Alliance (www.yogaalliance.org) has established training standards of at least two hundred training hours, with a specified number of hours in areas including techniques, teaching methodology, anatomy, physiology, and philosophy. The Yoga Alliance also registers schools that train students to the standards. Because some schools may meet the standards but not be registered, prospective students should check the requirements and decide if particular schools meet them. This is just one example; yoga training tends to be flexible to meet the needs of working adults. Some programs complete the training all in one session; others offer home study and internships once an initial training period is completed.

Typical topics covered in yoga training include:

Asanas (postures)	Meditation
Deep relaxation	Pranayama (breathing)
Body awareness	Guided imagery
Mind/body connection	Wellness and health
Spirit of yoga	Stress reduction
Yoga psychology	Prenatal yoga
Anatomy and physiology	Ayurveda
Chakras/energy centers	

Since all yoga programs are different, aspiring yoga teachers should research programs to find those that meet their needs. Never fear, however, because there is a yoga program for everyone, and finding the best one for you is just half the fun!

The success of a yoga teacher also depends on personal qualities and skills. Some yoga teachers have strengths in teaching the poses while others focus on developing a spiritual space for the class to relax in. Regardless of the focus of the class, teachers who believe in what they are doing and are enthusiastic and confident are the most successful. Physical fitness and strong communication and observation skills also are needed.

Salary and Job Outlook

Salaries for yoga teachers vary due to the range of employment options. Typically, yoga teachers charge $10 to $15 per person per class, so the amount earned depends on the number of students. Since most yoga teachers are running their own businesses, the earnings depend on the marketing ability of the instructor. It can take time to build a reputation and a business, but established yoga teachers earn a comfortable living. In general, however, government statistics estimate the median annual earnings of yoga instructors to be about $25,500. The middle 50 percent of those working earn between $17,400 and $40,000. The bottom 10 percent earn less than $14,500, and the top 10 percent earn $55,600 or more. Earnings of successful self-employed personal yoga instructors can be much higher. Yoga teachers also earn income from training other instructors, publishing books, and being involved in other career activities and employment. Although most people don't go into yoga for the money, teachers find their services are in demand.

The outlook for yoga teachers is promising as yoga becomes part of mainstream health and exercise and is covered by insurance companies. Increasing numbers of yoga instructors are finding employment in corporate and health care settings.

Professional Associations

American Yoga Association
www.americanyogaassociation.org

California Yoga Teachers Association
www.yogateachersassoc.org
(This association offers insurance coverage for yoga teachers and publishes *Yoga Journal* once a year.)

International Association of Yoga Therapists
www.iayt.org

Iyengar Yoga National Association of the United States
www.iynaus.org

Yoga Alliance
www.yogaalliance.org

Yoga Journal
www.yogajournal.com
(This journal provides a directory of yoga centers in the United States including training programs.)

Schools

For a comprehensive list of schools, visit the websites for *Yoga Journal* and the Yoga Alliance.

Center for Yoga
www.yogaworks.com

Integrative Yoga Therapy
www.iytyogatherapy.com

International Sivananda Yoga Vedanta Centers
www.sivananda.org

Kripalu Center
www.kripalu.org

The Naropa Institute
www.naropa.edu

13

Additional Holistic
Health Care Careers

The field of holistic health care is so vast that it would be impossible to cover all of the facets of it in one small book. Thus far, you've learned about the main areas of holistic health. In this chapter you'll learn about a couple of other segments of the holistic health care field, more marginal specialties, including ayurveda, biofeedback, feng shui, homeopathy, and iridology. This chapter is only meant to introduce you to these areas. If you find your interest piqued, you should conduct further research online or in your local library. No matter which area of holistic health you choose to pursue, you are sure to find a rewarding career.

Ayurveda

Ayurveda originated in India more than five thousand years ago. It is a spiritual healing science that combines spirituality and the laws of nature to heal illness, prevent disease, and increase longevity.

The word *ayurveda* means "the science of life and longevity" in Sanskrit. It is as much a religion as a healing science. Disease is believed to be a loss of faith in the Divine or a spiritual lacking, followed by poor digestion and weakened immune system. Healing takes the form of natural therapies to create balance in a person.

Ayurveda is based on the belief that all living things are a combination of energy elements: air, fire, and water. Ayurveda treatment is highly individualized and is based on the type of elements constituted in the body. All living things have predominately one or more of the energy elements. There are three primary energy types, or *doshas*: *vata*, *pitta*, and *kapha*. Classifying clients into their types is the first step toward treating health problems.

The vata type is associated with the element air. People of this type are typically thin, physically active, creative, and adaptable. When their dosha is out of balance they can have symptoms of worry, fear, anxiety, dry skin, constipation, and restlessness. Fire is the primary constitution of pitta types. When they are healthy they are warm, of medium build, and ambitious. They tend to have a healthy appetite and make strong leaders. When out of balance they are hot tempered, impatient, irritable, and prone to skin rashes, acne, ulcers, and disorders of the liver, kidney, heart, and spleen. Water or kapha types have well-developed bodies, thick wavy hair, and tend to move and speak slowly. They are calm, loyal, and happy. When unbalanced, kaphas may become greedy, overweight, and lethargic. They are prone to heart and kidney problems. Individuals usually have one dominant type or a combination of two types.

To diagnose the correct dosha, ayurvedic physicians ask questions, administer questionnaires, and observe their clients. Once the dosha is identified, an individualized treatment program is developed to balance the energy and treat health problems.

Ayurvedic physicians treat the whole person—mind, body, and spirit. They use only natural therapies such as herbs, nutrition, massage, yoga, exercise, aromatherapy, music therapy, sweat treatments, meditation, fasting, exercise, crystal and spiritual healing, and enemas for detoxifying the body. The dosha type is the guiding principle behind treatment, and certain foods are recommended for each type when it is out of balance.

Training and Qualifications

In India, training to become an ayurveda physician takes five years. There is nothing comparable to this in the United States. Currently ayurveda practitioners are not regulated or licensed, although you can find them working in the United States and find other health practitioners who use ayurveda principles. Each state has its own laws regarding what practitioners can do. Typically, as long as ayurvedic practitioners don't call themselves a doctor and don't "diagnose and treat" people, but rather "educate, analyze, and suggest," they can practice in most states. There are several schools that offer training programs for current health care practitioners or anyone else interested in ayurveda. These programs vary in length and intensity. Some offer two-year programs that lead to a certification as an ayurvedic practitioner. Others are shorter programs for people who want to incorporate ayurveda into their current method of care. Finally, some people study ayurveda for their own personal use and to maintain their health.

Professional Association

The Ayurvedic Institute
www.ayurveda.com

Schools

Ayurveda Holistic Center
www.ayurvedahc.com

Maharishi University of Management
www.mum.edu

Rocky Mountain Institute of Yoga and Ayurveda
www.rmiya.org

Biofeedback

Biofeedback is a treatment method to help clients control body functions. It utilizes clients' will, motivation, thoughts, behaviors, and feelings to improve health problems. It is a technique that uses the mind to control the body. Biofeedback therapists use devices or machines to provide information to a client about what is happening in his or her body. Devices often have beepers or flashing lights to indicate physical responses in the body (for example, a tone to indicate muscle tension). The purpose is to teach the client to control bodily functions that normally are not controlled. Biofeedback therapists teach clients to bring under control involuntary bodily processes such as heart rate, breathing, muscles, body temperature, psychological states, brain waves, blood pressure, and blood flow. For example, a stroke patient with a paralyzed leg can use biofeedback to recognize when the leg muscles are activated. This signal can be used to guide exercises and teach the client how it feels when the leg muscles are working. The client can then focus his or her efforts on increasing the signal of the machine—the more the machine flashes, the more the leg is working. Once control of the indicator is achieved, the client can learn to control body functions on his or her own.

Stress reduction and relaxation are key components of biofeedback therapy. Biofeedback therapists work to help clients change reactions to stress and teach them how to relax. For example, a client whose blood pressure goes up in stressful situations can be taught to control it in the face of stress or anxiety. Stress is believed to cause and contribute to many health problems, and biofeedback has been particularly successful with stress-related illnesses. It is used to treat migraine headaches, tension headaches, insomnia, hypertension, high/low blood pressure, cardiac abnormalities, digestive disorders, epilepsy, muscle spasms, anxiety, depression, sexual dysfunction, dental disorders, paralysis, movement disorders, and various types of pain.

Using therapeutic skills, technological devices, and instruction, biofeedback therapists teach clients to control their bodies. Biofeedback requires a client's motivation and effort, otherwise it does not work. Therapists often suggest diet and lifestyle changes in addition to biofeedback therapy. Biofeedback is not a cure but a tool for incorporating client motivation and control into the healing process.

Training and Qualifications

Many biofeedback practitioners are trained health care professionals who include biofeedback into their method of care. Biofeedback is used by physicians, psychologists, psychiatrists, social workers, dentists, nurses, physical therapists, rehabilitation counselors, internists, and relaxation specialists. Typically, individuals who become trained in biofeedback have some health care or science background.

There are no laws or licensing requirements governing biofeedback therapists. The Biofeedback Certification Institute of America (BCIA; www.bcia.org) certifies biofeedback practitioners who meet standards for practice, although certification is not legally required. To be certified, candidates must have a bachelor's degree in an approved health care field and complete biofeedback education, clinical training, and a written exam. Other training programs may offer certificate programs, but to be certified by BCIA, candidates must meet certification requirements.

Professional Associations

Association for Applied Psychophysiology and Biofeedback
www.aapb.org

Biofeedback Certification Institute of America
www.bcia.org

Schools

Biofeedback Institute of San Francisco
http://itsa.ucsf.edu

Southeastern Biofeedback Neurobehavioral Institute
www.eegfeedback.org

Stens Corporation
www.stens-biofeedback.com

Feng Shui

Feng shui is an ancient Chinese technique for bringing one's home, workplace, and outer surroundings into balance for optimal health and life circumstances. In Hong Kong some people will not work for a company unless the building is adjusted to feng shui principles. Many companies and individuals in the United States have begun using feng shui principles for designing their homes and offices. Similar to acupuncture where the focus of treatment is balancing the chi or life-force energy in the body, feng shui focuses on the life-force energy in our environment.

The premise of feng shui is that structures have energy that flows throughout living space. Blocked energy flow in a home or work space can cause health, financial, family, career, and interpersonal problems. Practitioners divide floor plans of living or work space into nine equal rectangles. Different areas of space relate to different areas of one's life. For example, the front entrance space relates to knowledge and career.

Once blockages in a room or space are determined, practitioners recommend changes to allow the energy to flow more freely. Some simple changes might include rearrangement of chairs, desks, couches, beds, and tables. For example, bed placement is important for health, strength, and mental peace. The bed should be arranged so that a person who is in it can see anyone entering through the bedroom door.

In designing space, feng shui practitioners consider structural factors such as placement of doors, stairs, hallways, angled ceilings, and beams. They would recommend against having the front door open up to a wall. This is viewed as inhibiting and cramping one's life. Mirrors are a common and inexpensive remedy for opening blocked passageways. Mirrors placed in narrow, dark, or other areas prevent the feeling of constriction. Some practitioners use mirrors specific to the client's problem (health mirrors, career mirrors, and so forth) and hang them in rooms that correspond to the client's problem. Through these and other inexpensive techniques, feng shui practitioners balance the flow of energy in a home or work space to increase positive energy, harmony, health, and happiness.

Training and Qualifications

There are several books available explaining feng shui principles to the public. Many people learn simple techniques for arranging their home or office through independent reading. For more advanced application, formal training is required. Many schools of natural healing or Chinese medicine offer courses in feng shui. Training can vary from a one-day workshop to a semester-long class. Feng Shui USA (www.fengshuiusa.com) provides a five-day intensive training program to become a feng shui consultant. Topics covered include a history of feng shui, feng shui analysis, use of color and the five elements, site evaluations, basic solutions, spiritual solutions, and setting up a consulting business. The Feng Shui Institute of America (www.windwater.com) also offers training programs. Feng shui is not regulated by state or federal licensing or certification laws. Typically training programs grant certificates of completion, but there are no regulated standards for the profession. Trained consultants are free to open up their own business.

Professional Associations

American Feng Shui Institute
www.amfengshui.com

Feng Shui Institute of America
www.windwater.com

Feng Shui USA
www.fengshuiusa.com

Homeopathy

Homeopathy is an alternative system of health care developed by Dr. Samual Hahnemann in the early nineteenth century. It is a common form of health care in England, France, Switzerland, Germany, India, and other countries and recently has had a resurgence of popularity in the United States. The cornerstone of homeopathic philosophy is the "law of similars"—meaning, let likes be cured by likes. The law of similars states that disease is cured by medicine that when taken by healthy people causes the same symptom. For example, substances that cause nausea in a healthy person can be used in infinitesimal doses to treat someone suffering from nausea.

Homeopaths identify patient symptoms by conducting extensive interviews to determine which homeopathic remedy best matches the patient's physical, mental, and emotional needs. Often a homeopath will prescribe only one or a small number of doses to give the body a chance to respond to the treatment using the least-invasive methods possible. The medicines are made from plants, minerals, and other natural substances. There are more than two thousand homeopathic remedies; they are made by diluting and shaking small amounts of homeopathic substances several times over. In fact, the more the remedy has been diluted, the stronger it is believed to be. The goal is to use remedies to support the body's natural healing abilities.

Similar to other holistic practitioners, homeopaths use a whole-person approach to working with patients. They are interested in many areas of a person's life—the physical, mental, and spiritual. They view symptoms as a sign that the body needs help rather than as something to suppress, and they try to treat underlying causes of the symptoms. Homeopathy has been particularly effective with chronic diseases, long-term physical and emotional problems, recurring conditions, and conditions that have not been helped by traditional medicine.

Training and Qualifications

There is some confusion over who can practice homeopathic medicine. According to the National Center for Homeopathy (www .homeopathic.org), to practice homeopathy in the United States, one must be a licensed health care provider. Only medical doctors (M.D.s) and osteopathic physicians (D.O.s) are licensed to diagnose and treat illnesses and use homeopathy. In many states, other health care providers such as naturopathic physicians, nurse practitioners, physician assistants, dentists, veterinarians, chiropractors, acupuncturists, and nurse midwives are allowed to practice homeopathy under the scope of their licenses.

The issue appears to be over how homeopathic remedies are used. Of course, only licensed health care providers are allowed to diagnose and treat disease, but there are many other homeopaths practicing homeopathy under the role of consultant, adviser, and/or educator. Rather than diagnose and treat a problem, they analyze and suggest remedies for symptoms. This leaves the field of homeopathy wide open to individuals who are interested in pursuing it as a profession. There are a number of programs of study available to both health care practitioners and non-health-care practitioners. The profession is unregulated and there are no licensing or set standards of practice. Most schools award certificates of completion. Finally, many individual consumers learn about and use homeopathic remedies themselves. Most remedies can be purchased over the counter at health food stores, and there is a wide variety of books on the subject.

Professional Associations

Homeopathic Academy of Naturopathic Physicians
www.hanp.net

National Center for Homeopathy
www.homeopathic.org

North American Society of Homeopaths
www.homeopathy.org

Schools

American University of Complementary Medicine
www.aucm.org

Bastyr University
www.bastyr.edu

Caduceus Institute of Classical Homeopathy
www.homeopathyhome.com/caduceus

Hahnemann College of Homeopathy
www.hahnemanncollege.com

Homeopathy School of Colorado
www.homeopathyschool.org

Institute of Classical Homeopathy
www.classicalhomoeopathy.org

International Academy of Classical Homeopathy
www.classicalhomeopathy.com

National College of Naturopathic Medicine
www.ncnm.edu

chool of Homeopathy

School of Natural Therapeutics
t.org

New York Luminos School of Homeopathy
www.nyhomeopathy.com

Northwestern Academy of Homeopathy
www.homeopathicschool.org

Pacific Academy of Homeopathy
www.homeopathy-academy.org

San Diego Homeopathic Education and Training
www.homeopathic-academy.com

Teleosis School of Homeopathy
www.teleosisschool.org

Iridology

Iridology is the study of the eye and iris to determine an individual's strengths and weaknesses and to diagnose health problems. It was developed in the late 1800s by a Hungarian doctor, Ignatz Von Peczely.

Iridology is primarily a diagnostic tool rather than a method of treatment for health problems. It is believed that signs of ill health are seen in the eyes before other symptoms appear and that specific characteristics in the iris can point to health problems. By using iris charts, iridologists map and create a blueprint of a client's genetic, physical, and emotional constitution. The eye is connected to our brain and body through the nervous system, and the iris is made up of more than twenty-eight hundred nerve endings. Iridologists have developed charts identifying areas in the iris that correspond to major organ systems and regions in the body. They use photography and magnifying equipment to closely examine a client's iris. During the exam, they look for colors, patterns, shapes, lines, rings, inflammations, lesions, and flecks. They examine the fiber quality and graininess of the iris. Information from an iris reading can reveal a variety of health problems. For example, by using an iris chart, a dark rim around the iris can indicate a problem with the elimination of toxins. It can show the strengths and weaknesses of organs and systems, nutritional needs, inflammation, allergies, toxicity, and the predisposition to certain health problems. Iridologists are not legally allowed to diagnose specific diseases (such as cancer, diabetes, or Alzheimer's disease) unless they have a medical license, but they can point to areas of weaknesses in the body.

The diagnostic information from an iridology reading is used for preventing illness and disease. If clients are aware of their physiological weaknesses, they can prevent predisposed illnesses by making lifestyle changes. This information combined with other diagnostic tools can be used to refer clients to additional health care, if needed. Iridology is a safe, noninvasive, nontoxic, painless, inexpensive, and quick method of analysis.

Training and Qualifications

There are no licensing requirements for becoming an iridologist. Training primarily takes the form of a certificate program. The National Iridology Research Association (part of the International Iridology Practitioners Association; www.iridologyassn.org) offers a certificate program that awards the degree of Certified Iridologist. Other classes can be found offered at schools for holistic health and healing or as part of training programs for other holistic health occupations. Iridology is often used as a supplemental diagnostic tool by acupuncturists, naturopaths, herbalists, nutritionists, energy healers, and other holistic care practitioners.

Professional Association

International Iridology Practitioners Association
www.iridologyassn.org

About the Author

GILLIAN TIERNEY SERVED as the assistant director of career and employment services at Saint Anselm College in Manchester, New Hampshire. As a career development specialist, she counseled clients on the many career options available. She became interested in holistic health care through her personal use of alternative therapies and study of yoga. Since leaving Saint Anselm College, she entered the field of human resources, in which she is currently serving as the director of human resources at Bottomline Technologies in Portsmouth, New Hampshire. Her interest in health and wellness extends into this corporate setting, and she is proud to have brought weekly, lunchtime yoga to Bottomline, as well as an annual health and wellness month. She earned her bachelor's degree from the University of New Hampshire, Durham, and her M.Ed./C.A.G.S. in counseling psychology from the University of Massachusetts, Amherst.